To Becky
God bless you.

Brokenness
to Beauty

*Transforming Your Brokenness
into a Beautiful Life*

Jacqueline Wallace
Hebrews 10:'24

Jacqueline Wallace

WESTBOW
PRESS®
A DIVISION OF THOMAS NELSON
& ZONDERVAN

WestBow Press books may be ordered through booksellers or by contacting:

WestBow Press
A Division of Thomas Nelson & Zondervan
1663 Liberty Drive
Bloomington, IN 47403
www.westbowpress.com
1 (866) 928-1240

Cover images property of author.

ISBN: 978-1-5127-1974-1 (sc)
ISBN: 978-1-5127-1973-4 (hc)
ISBN: 978-1-5127-1972-7 (e)

Library of Congress Control Number: 2015918866

Print information available on the last page.

WestBow Press rev. date: 12/29/2015

Contents

Foreword

Into every life suffering will come. This world is terribly broken, and that brokenness affects every inhabitant and system. We could say that the world has an immune system that has been degraded by toxins built up over a lifetime.

Not only do we face assaults on our physical bodies, but sin has been passed on from one generation to the next, increasing wickedness. People inflict injustices, small and great, upon each other. Unimaginable horrors are perpetrated upon vulnerable children, the elderly, and the weak. There are more millions enslaved in our generation than at any other time in human history. Without the Almighty holding back evil and guiding us through this dangerous journey, we could only despair.

Jesus was asked by his disciples about the end of this age of misery. In the minds of his closest followers he had come to set everything right—right away. But he painted a bleak picture in response to their questions, describing a future characterized by the increase in earthquakes, wars, diseases, persecution, and inhumane coldheartedness. These are birth pains, he said, before the birth of his kingdom.

Jesus told his disciples not to fear because "this gospel of the kingdom will be preached in the whole world ... and after that the end will come" (Matthew 24:14). This was not what they wanted to hear. And when we suffer, it is not what we want to hear either. The big picture may seem so detached from our daily challenges that we hardly know how to connect the two. Even so, the followers of Jesus are to focus on the big picture of God's purposes.

When I first met the author of this book, I was an unsaved teen. From our first encounter, I sensed that here was a person who connected the big picture of God's ultimate purposes with her own daily challenges and suffering. That connection was quite mysterious to me. She could not project her voice or articulate clearly due to her weakness. The girl did not waste words. There was something about her focus and economy of words that made me and others lean in to listen to what she had to say.

It was obvious that she had been distilled from hollow perspectives to focus on what truly matters. Most of us hope to learn to connect divine purposes to our daily lives without the suffering part. That will not happen. Everyone suffers—or borrows the sufferings of others willingly. God knows how to both reduce our perspective and nurture us into focusing on his great heart, his great purposes, through the daily assaults, challenges, and weaknesses we face. Oh, how we need to embrace his offers of divine help as we make this journey!

One of the great joys along the journey is that there are people, like Jacque, who have gone ahead of us, shedding light on what really matters. Her raw honesty helps us turn from fear toward confidence in God, from brokenness to reflecting the beauty of our Savior and Shepherd, the Lord Jesus. Lean in and learn.

Michele Rickett
President and Founder of She Is Safe
Co-author of *Daughters of Hope* and *Forgotten Girls*

Acknowledgments

"I think you should blog about your cancer journey. You have something to say that can help others, so I set up a blog for you." My husband's encouragement sometimes took the form of a gentle nudge, causing me to take stutter-steps forward into brave new worlds of endeavor. I never in a thousand years would have imagined, let alone pursued, blogging my struggles as I went through breast cancer treatment!

But Randy had. Having been married to me for over thirty years by the time of my cancer diagnosis, he knew that what I had learned from living with a debilitating disease all of my adult life would inform my walk through this current crisis. He knew these valuable lessons could benefit others if I'd only share them.

So he cleared the path for me to do just that by setting up a blog, something I knew nothing about. This became the platform from which I could talk about my journey through the swirling waters of breast cancer.

Jacque's Journey was my first blog, the one in which I shared my cancer journey week by week during that year and a half of treatment, which included two surgeries, two sets of chemotherapy, and a course of radiation. It was therapeutic for me to write down my thoughts and feelings, and apparently Randy was right that I had something valuable to say to others, because as I wrote, comments started coming back to me. Then readers started asking me when I was going to write a book.

I am grateful to all the people who encouraged me to write: my husband, Randy, who is still my most persistent encourager; our sons and daughters-in-law; our extended family members; our friends; and readers of my blog. Had they not spurred me on, I never would have undertaken this project.

Many ladies kindly made room in their lives to read all or parts of the manuscript. They helped me see through their eyes. First was my writers critique group, who read and critiqued several portions: Bethane Banks, Donna Hudson, Mikie Pyle, Sharon Miller, and Nancy Clover. Then I asked several friends to be beta readers, and they read and gave input: Rose Anderson, Melinda Bianco, Jenny Evans, Wendy Hammond, Amber Hayes, Jana Kolthoff, and Elise Leiss. Thank you, girls!

My sister-in-law, Michele Rickett, herself a published author, gave me a nudge while Randy and I were visiting their home over Thanksgiving one year. Her words finally catapulted me into writing the first draft. Michele graciously wrote the foreword to *Brokenness to Beauty*. Thank you, sis.

A big thank-you goes to my editor, Rachel Starr Thomson, for all her guidance, encouragement, and expert advice to shape and hone my manuscript, readying it for publication. I believe the book is much better for her knowledgeable and insightful editorial work.

I'm sure I've missed someone who deserves thanks, but I hope they know I am grateful for all the encouragement and support I have received on this journey. God especially has been patient with me, allowing me the time to work through all the ups and downs of accomplishing this task. In the final analysis, I wrote this book because I believe he wanted me to. May he be pleased and glorified through it.

Introduction

How do you handle traumatic news? How do you move through each day when it feels like your old familiar world is crumbling around you? Is it possible, and if so how, to live joyfully and confidently while assailed by pain, fear, or devastating loss?

As I contemplated and prayed about what I would say in a book about going through suffering—and getting through it whole and better than when one started the journey—it became clear to me that several principles are of vital importance, both for those who are going through trials and for those who walk alongside them. These principles became the framework upon which I sculpted the body of this book.

My journey in dealing with life's difficulties began not with breast cancer at age fifty-seven but with myasthenia gravis (MG), a debilitating and often life-threatening disease, diagnosed when I was fifteen years old. Part 1, therefore, travels back in time to my youth, where my life lessons in struggle and suffering started. Like a stone skipping along the surface of a lake, this section touches on points in my life up to the day I heard the frightening news that I had breast cancer.

What informs and shapes our responses to trials? How does that make a difference in the way we move through them? As I analyzed how I cope with hard times and traumatic events, I realized how much the Bible has influenced the way I live. In Part 2, we will explore this first principle: the importance of the Bible to our lives.

Most people at some point—usually when they feel helpless and in great need of something or Someone beyond themselves—pray. What is prayer? Does prayer make a difference in our lives, both in crisis times and ordinary days, or is it just noise in the air? Whistling in the dark? How significant is prayer to one going through suffering of any sort? In Part 3 we consider these questions and realities about prayer.

Misery may love company, but sufferers definitely need it. We all need other people to help and support us in times of suffering and trial. In Part 4, we take a look at the importance of a community of support for those who are going through difficult times.

Finally, in Part 5, I challenge us to take a look beyond what our eyes can see to that which our hearts can perceive: an eternal perspective that gives us what we need to live above the pain and suffering of this life and do so with joy and peace. When you are down it can sometimes be hard to get up, even literally hard to drag yourself out of bed in the morning. But when we have a reason to get up, it helps propel us even on our darkest days. What purpose could be so compelling as to give us resolve in the throes of suffering? I'll tackle this question in the final part of the book.

Many excellent books have been written about aspects of suffering and living life in the midst of it. On the Resources page, I have compiled a short list of valuable books and online helps for additional reading in hopes that these may further encourage you in your own journey. You can also read my original blog, detailing my cancer journey, at http:// jacquesjourney.blogspot.com, or visit my current blog at https://brokennesstobeauty.wordpress.com.

Most of our days are filled with activities that pull us in many directions at once; therefore, this book is structured so that it may be read in short sections, easily adapted to a busy lifestyle. It is my hope that I have written these few chapters simply and clearly enough so that those who read it may, as with the vision given to Habakkuk, "read it fluently," or with understanding, so that they may go on in their life journey stronger for it and in turn share it with others (Habakkuk 2:2).

Part 1

My Story

Chapter 1

Then to Now

"I have the diagnosis. It is breast cancer." The doctor's words hit me like a stomach punch, taking my breath away. I had the urge to turn and look over my shoulder to see who he was talking to; certainly not me! My mind reeled, simultaneously rejecting and absorbing the news:

I have cancer.

I recalled another doctor, many years earlier, saying almost the same words when I was just fifteen: "I know the diagnosis." The doctor told my parents I had a rare disease called myasthenia gravis. It sapped my strength and energy: in one year I deteriorated from an energetic teenager into a listless one. Constantly weak and tired, I had increasing difficulty talking, chewing, swallowing, and keeping my eyelids open. It was hard to grip things with my hands, lift my arms to comb my hair, or carry my schoolbooks. My arms felt like lead weights.

At night in bed I secretly cried, asking God what was wrong with me. Why wasn't my body working right? It felt like a rusty suit of armor enclosed me, weighing me down so that I couldn't move freely. I wasn't imagining the drooping eyelids, my inability to talk and eat and use my hands, arms, and legs . . . was I? Was I going crazy?

My parents weren't home as much as they used to be, so while they observed some unusual changes in me, they were not aware of all the symptoms of weakness I routinely endured. Mom had taken a job at the hospital to help support the family while Dad completed his surgical residency. He lived at the hospital more than at home, it seemed. So they were unaware of my fear of climbing onto a chair or step because I had fallen and hit my head, my leg and neck muscles too weak to support me. They had no idea how I struggled to open a dresser drawer because my hands couldn't grip the knobs. When they observed me choking on food because I was too weak to swallow, however, they became alarmed and started taking me to doctors to find out what was wrong.

I hadn't always been tired and weak. Living in the country as a young girl, I remember tromping through the woods behind our house (I must have made enough noise to scare away all the snakes for miles around; thankfully I never saw one on my forays). We kids had a rope-and-tire swing hung from a tree on the edge of a bank that dropped off into the woods, and we'd soar Tarzan-like out over the open space and back around to our starting point.

Unless, that is, our trajectory was too short and we hit the tree on our return instead of our intended landing point! I loved horseback riding and playing in the creek that ran through the eighty acres of our land. I didn't play much with dolls, although I naturally watched out for my little brother, who was nine years younger than me. My mother's mantra to the four of us kids, "Go outside and play!," surely contributed to my tomboyishness and love of the outdoors.

At about age thirteen, after the family moved to the big city so my doctor dad could pursue his studies, my once carefree life changed. Symptoms of muscle weakness brought on physical struggles and emotional distress. Not knowing what is wrong with you is torture. For two years I lived in this no-man's land while the weakness increased.

When I finally heard the doctor's diagnosis, rather than fear, I felt relief! I wasn't crazy! There was a reason for my weakness and exhaustion: I had a *disease* with a *name!* Strange comfort, perhaps, but oh, very real.

The next few months became a blur of hospitalizations, tests, and adjustment to medications, which sometimes had unpleasant or embarrassing side effects. Instead of getting stronger, however, I grew weaker and more debilitated. Within six months of my diagnosis I didn't have the strength to go to school, feed myself, or lift my arms to comb my hair. I became bed bound. My symptoms of extreme weakness were a type of semiparalysis, so any activity was a struggle and produced exhaustion.

Back to the hospital I went again, this time for two weeks of bed rest. Then my parents made the major decision to allow a surgical procedure called a thymectomy. The surgeon would break my sternum (breastbone), open up my chest, and remove the thymus gland, which lies above the heart. The thymus, like the appendix, is thought to be part of the immune system but usually shrivels up as we get older. For unknown reasons mine was enlarged, as some myasthenics' are. Removing the thymus seemed to help some MG patients, but there were no guarantees the surgery would help me.

The doctor also told my parents that in my condition, the prospects were slim that I would survive the surgery. But she felt it was worth the risk because the way I was deteriorating, I wasn't going to live long without some change. I would either continue to weaken and succumb because of the inability to breathe, or I would choke to death. The slightest infection would quickly kill me. My body was not responding to conventional treatment with medications, and there were no other options available for me, no other options for my parents to choose from.

Looking back, I cannot begin to imagine my parents' agony. The closest I can come was when my eight-year-old son was hit by a car while riding his bicycle. What a nightmare! Later that day, after several tests, we learned he had no serious injuries; he was fine, just some road rash. His helmet took the brunt of the collision with the windshield of the car. God had mercifully spared him.

My parents, however, watched me decline from a healthy, active teenager to a shadow of their child, fading from this life day by day. The prognosis was grim. Little hope was given them for my recovery.

I remember sitting in the hospital bed, my parents and the doctors in the room asking me my opinion about the proposed surgery. Was I willing to go through it? I don't remember all they told me, only that this surgery might help me. I gave my assent almost cheerfully. My optimistic nature, coupled with ignorance of my real condition, made me hopeful I'd get better. What could I lose? Little did I know.

A few days later I awoke from surgery with an elephant sitting on my chest. Well, it felt that way! Though I don't think I'd ever before taken anything stronger than an aspirin, I was glad for the "big guns" of pain medication. I had a raw, eight-inch incision down my chest, with tubes protruding from under my rib cage: one for the left lung, one for the right.

My dad stood next to my bed, a different kind of pain etched on his face. When I tried to speak, I discovered I couldn't. I had a hole in my throat, a tracheostomy, he explained, with a tube that connected to a breathing machine. It pumped air into my lungs, breathing for me since I couldn't breathe on my own. I wrote notes or made hand motions instead of talking. I quickly learned the frustration of not being able to clearly and simply communicate verbally.

For weeks I floated in and out of consciousness in the ICU, those tubes protruding from my lungs and the hole in my throat. Finally, after what I thought was a couple of weeks, I was released from the hospital and taken home. Years later, in a conversation with my mom, I learned I had been in the ICU for six weeks. I was shocked! I had no idea I'd been there that long.

Then Mom told me what went on during those long weeks when they sat by my bedside while I drifted in and out of consciousness. I almost died, she said. I declined daily. The doctors had anticipated this from the outset, and they tried to prepare my parents. They were doing everything medically feasible. Lots of people prayed for me, many of whom I had never met.

Then the night came when the doctors didn't think I'd live to see the morning. Dad, who had been "wrestling" with God for weeks to save his little girl, finally gave up the fight, telling God to do with me as he pleased.

That night, Mom said, was the turning point in my recovery. I did live through the night, and following that, I steadily improved until I finally came home from the hospital. I weighed eighty-seven pounds. I recuperated over the summer and entered high school in the fall to catch up on courses I had missed the previous year. Unable to carry a full load of classes, I had to spread them over an extra year. I graduated with honors three years later, squeezing four years of high school into five.

The surgery had been successful to a great degree. I was not cured of MG; there is no known cure to this day. But I was alive and functioning once again—not on the level of someone without MG, but doing amazingly well for me.

After graduating high school, I went to college. My parents took a big step of faith in allowing me to move several states away and live on a college campus. A cold or flu could precipitate a life-threatening myasthenic crisis in which I would become so weak I could not talk, swallow, or breathe. This crisis usually meant hospitalization and life support, i.e., a tube down my nose or throat so I could breathe with a machine's help. My parents risked not being there to help me if I got sick, yet they did not hold me back from pursuing my life goals. I loved life and refused to let physical limitations keep me from living joyfully, so I pushed through the difficulties. I went to a Bible college in Florida and there met Randy, who would become my husband. We were married while in college, and in the next few years I gave birth to two healthy sons.

Miracles to us, miracles all! That I could marry, bear children, and raise a family was and is miraculous to us. There were times, indeed, when I could barely function: hands too weak to pin a diaper, arms too weak to lift my baby, eyes too weak to safely drive because of double vision. Randy took over much of the care of our boys when they were toddlers, and his office was located in our home. He bathed and dressed our sons, cleaned house, and cooked. He took the boys out on his day off each week so I could have a break and rest. They made lots of memories together doing dad and son stuff.

There were trying times though. One evening Randy took me to a hospital ER because I was getting weaker by the hour. We guessed I had a flu bug again. I weakened to the point of not being able to talk, swallow, or breathe well. I was admitted to an ICU and on the way, when my throat filled with fluid, I began drowning in my own secretions because I was too weak to swallow.

Choking, trying to get a breath, in my mind's eye I saw Peter walking on the water, then Peter *in* the water, choking and crying out, "Lord, save me!" That was all I could cry out, over and over from my mind and heart: "Lord, save me! Lord, save me!" I knew if God didn't save me, I would die right there on that gurney.

Thank God someone realized I couldn't breathe. They intubated me right there in the hallway, putting the breathing tube down my throat into my airway without anesthesia; I was fully conscious. Although this procedure was extremely scary and unpleasant, I knew it was my only hope of surviving the ordeal. They finally got the tube into my airway. I could breathe. Blessed breath!

My in-control but distraught husband averted widowerhood that night. He could stop forming the words to tell his little boys that their mommy had died.

I was in the ICU for ten days on life support and gradually got over the flu that had so devastated my strength.

That was my last full-blown myasthenic crisis. We thank God he brought me through it and pray it will remain my last crisis!

I acknowledge that I should not be alive today, and not just from these ordeals. Many times I have come close to death, but God has brought me through each time. I have struggled with weakness every day of my life for nearly fifty years, but I have continued to live life to the fullest. In the hard times I learned to call on God daily, even moment by moment, for my strength: my physical, emotional, and spiritual strength.

Fast-forward forty-two years from the time of my MG diagnosis. The unwanted, frightening news of breast cancer had just been dumped on me, cancer that could kill me. Now all the life lessons I'd learned over the years needed to be pulled forward to meet this challenge head-on.

It is out of these life experiences I write. The nineteenth-century missionary Amy Carmichael, who herself lived many years with debilitating illness, used to remind her editors that what God "gives is never for ourselves alone but is given to be shared."[1] I believe she was right. My life path is not one I would have chosen, but since it has been my life and I have learned much as I've lived it, I want to share, in the pages of this book, what God has been teaching me.

Part 2

The Bible

Chapter 2

Finding Hope

*"The grass withers, the flower fades, but
the word of our God stands forever."*
Isaiah 40:8

Opening my Bible, I turned to the next psalm
in my daily reading, which began, "Praise the
LORD! I will give thanks to the LORD with all my heart"
(Psalm 111:1). And my heart said, "No, I don't want
to; I don't feel like praising God. I'd rather demand
to know why this is happening to me. Someone just
dumped a heavy weight on me, a weight that could
kill me, and I definitely do not like it. I sure don't
feel like giving thanks!"

Two days after I received a diagnosis of breast
cancer, I sat in the bedroom of our son's home in
California, nearly three thousand miles from our
home in West Virginia. Randy and I had stopped at
the doctor's office on our way to the airport to get

the results of my biopsy. We were heading west to spend Christmas and New Year's with our children and grandchildren. We'd been anticipating this time with great delight; it is hard to be a continent away from the ones you love most in the world. Now, in addition to absorbing and managing the news of cancer for ourselves, we had to share it with our sons and their wives—during the Christmas season!

As I read the psalm that morning, hurt, confusion, anger, and fear steamrolled through my head and heart. Yet simultaneously I acknowledged, "Yes, I will praise the LORD, because it is what I must do." All the more so because I was hurt and didn't want to do it.

I already knew how important it is that I *do* praise God in the face of conflicting, dark feelings. This is one of the major lessons of a life of suffering. If I praise God in life's sunny meadows, when circumstances seem nice and comfortable, but refuse to praise him in the dark valleys where fear and pain stalk, I make myself a hypocrite. Besides, it makes no sense to turn my back on God, cutting off my only source of comfort and strength and hope when I most need them.

At that moment I chose to praise God, a sheer act of the will. Quite frankly, my emotions were not on board yet! I struggled with the decision to do it. But I knew that if I chose according to my feelings at that moment, I'd end up in the depths of despair and would have a long, hard battle to dig myself out of that pit. This was not academic head knowledge. I had been on the edge of that dark pit of depression many times, so I knew from experience not to go there.

When I decided to praise God, I chose to submit to his sovereignty in my life, just like my dad did when he gave me up to God. The Bible played a key role in that initial decision and others that followed, my emotions trailing along behind. The Bible served as a rock, a stabilizer for my life, protecting me from being tossed about by my mind and emotions, especially in this time of distress.

> For whatever was written in earlier times was written for our instruction, so that through perseverance and encouragement of the Scriptures we might have hope. (Romans 15:4)

I have learned that these two things, *perseverance* and *encouragement of the Scriptures*, are important factors in getting through tough times. The Scriptures are full of encouragement because they are about God's dealings with people, people just like you and me. I wrote this in my blog after my first surgery for cancer:

> What is hopeless and impossible with man is not so for God, for all things are possible with God. Am I scared? Of course I am. Do I have anger and fears? Absolutely. I cry to the Lord who hears and understands, and who alone can do anything about them. I cast myself on his mercy. If others hadn't been in similar situations we wouldn't have the Scriptures,

which are full of such agonies. Now I choose to affirm my faith in the God Who Is.

Over the years I had learned to press on no matter how hard it became, even in the face of not knowing how things might turn out. But I leaned hard on God and his Word. The encouragement of the Scriptures is available to all, but it only comes from reading (or hearing) the Scriptures.

I continued reading through the Psalms after my cancer diagnosis. I had made reading Scripture a part of my life for many years at that point, because I learned long ago the power of the Word of God to affect my life in positive ways. I opened my Bible eager to learn from God. In it, I read about what others experienced down through the centuries, many of them in much worse circumstances than mine. I read how God was present with them and helped those who trusted in him. And I gained encouragement in the midst of my scary situation.

When I persevered through trials and gained encouragement from the Scriptures, God produced hope in me. If we give up, quit, fail to persevere in our struggles, we become hopeless. By hearing what God had to say through his Word, I found courage to go on. When I did that, my hope was renewed.

Many people have commented on how strong I am. Let me be the first to say that I am not strong; I am not a rock of strength. I go *to* the Rock: Jesus Christ. He is my strength. He is the Son of God, my Savior. I cry out to him in prayer and listen to him speak to me in the Bible, and in these ways I find strength and comfort and the encouragement I need to persevere. From this I gain hope. I find grace and strength to help me get through each day.

I wrote in my blog:

> Today I begin chemotherapy. I am nervous, apprehensive, I do admit. Lord, take my fears and anxious thoughts. I need your peace now. "But I am afflicted and in pain; may Your salvation, O God, set me securely on high. I will praise the name of God with song and magnify Him with thanksgiving. And it will please the Lord better than an ox or a young bull with horns and hoofs. The humble have seen it and are glad; you who seek God, let your heart revive. For the Lord hears the needy" (Psalm 69:29–33).

And God gave me peace.

Chapter 3

Foundations

When I was a child, my dad and my uncles sometimes got together and built a shed or garage, pouring concrete for foundation footers. This work fascinated me. They would pull out their tools and commence man tasks: measuring to fine detail, hammering, sawing, drilling, and mixing concrete. It was loud man talk and sweat and hard labor, these men working together. Their work completed, they'd smile and joke and backslap one another, knowing they'd done a good job.

Watching them, I learned about laying a solid foundation so a structure can be built securely on top of it. This in turn helped me grasp the truth of building a good foundation for my life. I understood better what Jesus meant about a house built on the rock:

> Therefore, everyone who hears these words of mine and acts on them, may be compared to

a wise man who built his house on the rock. And the rain fell, and the floods came, and the winds blew and slammed against that house; and yet it did not fall, for it had been founded on the rock. (Matthew 7:24)

According to Jesus, hearing and putting his words into practice guarantees a strong life. It is not just hearing the Word but doing what is heard that makes a strong life, one which will weather the storms and floods.

Growing up, I learned about God by being taught the Scriptures in Sunday school and church, at home, and in Vacation Bible Schools and summer Bible camps. From the Bible I learned that Jesus died on the cross, taking on himself the sin of us all. He rose from the tomb and ascended to heaven to sit at God the Father's right hand, having made provision for our salvation and the forgiveness of our sins. Then he sent his Spirit to live in those who trust in him, giving us the ability to live a new life in his power. Having put my faith in Jesus as a child, even when I was alone in my hospital room as a young teenager I never felt alone. I knew he was with me (John 14:16–17).

Foundations were laid in my life, strong foundations rooted in the Bible, upon which I have been building ever since—seeking to put Jesus's words into practice, allowing God to do his work in me. Though I haven't done it perfectly, I am still pursuing that way of life as a learner of Jesus (Philippians 3:12–16). And to this point, my life has stood through many storms, just as he said.

My routine of reading the Scriptures, which I continued throughout cancer treatment, stood me in good stead by continually getting me back into the Word of God. The Scriptures nurtured me daily, calling me back to the foundation of my life, giving me not only encouragement and hope but perspective. They acted like a compass, guiding me through the wind and waves of the storm in which I found myself. Even when I couldn't see farther than my own hand, so to speak, the compass of God's Word enabled me to continue to move in the right direction, in hope and trust in the Lord. The Scriptures gave me that which was beyond myself, beyond my limited vision and understanding.

A life pattern of reading Scripture starts with the conviction that the Bible is worth our time because it is the Word of God to us. We don't "find" time to read it; we make time. Since I am a morning person, early morning is the ideal time for me to spend in the Word. I carve it out, make it happen, and guard it jealously. Search out the time that is best for you. Make it happen and guard it. I am not legalistic about this—that is, my intent is not to shut out people or responsibilities. Rather, I make a priority of shutting myself in with the most important Person in my life: God. I am determined to make Bible reading a priority in order to hear him.

Some people ask, "Where do I start reading?" All Scripture is valuable, so I believe in going through all the books of the Bible. However, if you are new to reading Scripture, start with one of the gospels, like the gospel of John in the New Testament.

The best way to get to know God is by becoming acquainted with his Son, Jesus Christ. He told his questioning disciples, "Whoever has seen me has seen the Father" (John 14:9, ESV). I have found reading the Psalms and Proverbs to be of great value for practical Christian living. Regardless of what other book of the Bible I'm reading, on a daily basis I first read a psalm, fine-tuning my heart to focus on the Lord. There is no better way to start my day than by praising God. The Psalms are also a good source for learning about who God is and what he's done. When I work through to Psalm 150, I start again with Psalm 1. I've read and reread through Proverbs the same way. Talk about wisdom for everyday life!

And no, I've never been bored by repeating a psalm, a chapter of Proverbs, or any other book of the Bible! The Author is much smarter than I am, and because he is infinite, I can learn from God every time I open my Bible.

In an online or brick-and-mortar Bible bookstore you can find plans for reading through the entire Bible. I have friends who play Scripture CDs and listen to the Word at home or in their cars. They've listened through the whole Bible numerous times.

Currently I use the NASB and NIV regularly, but there are many other translations available today. Some are good for readability and others for deeper study. If you are new to Bible reading, I would suggest one of the more dynamic language versions, like the NIV or *The Living Bible*. For deeper study, I use the NASB. The ESV is a reliable version as well.

You could ask for assistance at a Bible bookstore for choosing the version best suited to your needs.

Just as my garden shed holds tools for gardening, I have a bookshelf of tools for Bible study. A good concordance, English dictionary, and Bible dictionary are tremendous helps as I look up verses and passages or learn what Bible terms and concepts mean. These study tools can even be found online. On the Resources page, I include links to some I use.

If you want to rototill rather than simply use a shovel in your studies, so to speak, try word studies in the original languages of the Bible. I love my *Interlinear for the Rest of Us: The Reverse Interlinear New Testament Word Studies* by William D. Mounce (see the Resources page). You don't need to know Greek to use it. I can look up a verse or passage in English and discover the Greek word or words underneath it, along with what they mean and how they are used in other verses.

If I use a commentary to see what someone who has studied the original languages of the Bible has to say, I am very careful about who I read and always remember that their words are those of a mere person; an individual's understanding is limited. The Word of God always has the final say.

In Bible college, one of our professors always had the students recite this verse as our prayer before class. It changed my perspective on how I should approach the Scriptures:

> Open my eyes, that I may behold wonderful things from Your law. (Psalm 119:18)

God himself, by his Holy Spirit living in us, is our teacher (1 Corinthians 2:10–13). Searching out a time, place, and tools for Bible study, and then sticking with it—not legalistically but out of love for God, preparing our hearts to hear him so that we can learn and do what he says—is the best way I know to "grow in the grace and knowledge of our Lord and Savior Jesus Christ" (2 Peter 3:18). When the storms of life come, there is no stronger foundation.

Chapter 4

God Calls Us

Traumatic interruptions in life—cancer or other illnesses, economic reversals, the suffering and death of loved ones, abandonment and divorce, persecution for one's faith, you name the struggle—can be doorways to greater understanding and growth when we allow God to turn our *devastation* into *education*. He is always calling to us. It's up to us to respond.

When I found myself flat on my face before God, knocked flat by the blow of cancer, I realized there was no one else to go to but God. I cried out to him and humbled my heart before him, and an amazing thing happened. The whole tenor of my experience began to change from despair to hope as God taught me and drew me close to himself.

> It is good for me that I was afflicted, that I may learn Your statutes. (Psalm 119:71)

Marj, a friend of mine, learned this. A few of us ladies sat in her living room chatting as we waited for the start of our prayer time together. Marj related in her warm way that she and her husband had been happily married for many years, and since they had no children, their world revolved around the two of them. As she put it, "It was Bill, God, and me." Then Bill was diagnosed with cancer. They bravely fought it together, Marj by Bill's side through it all. They prayed and asked God to bring Bill's healing. But it didn't come. My friend lost the love of her life. She was cast upon the Lord—alone.

Four years later, as we sat in her living room, Marj smiled and said with a twinkle in her eye, "You know, it used to be Bill, God, and me. Now I look up and say, 'Sorry, Bill, God's first now. He's taken over your place.'" I think Bill is in heaven smiling. Marj is growing in her relationship with God because she had nowhere else to go for comfort and strength in her grief. And he was there for her.

I've always been somewhat of a worrier. I tend to fret over things, tumbling them over and over in my mind. Through the years, as I've read the Bible, I couldn't help but read verses that state "do not worry, do not be fearful, do not fret, do not be anxious." These truths were in my head, but I was still a worrier.

During cancer treatment days, I dealt with all kinds of fears. There were always decisions to make and scary situations to face. I distinctly remember a day when the well-known verses Paul wrote to the

Philippians, verses I had memorized, finally took root in my heart and bore fruit:

> Be anxious for nothing, but in everything by prayer and supplication with thanksgiving let your requests be made known to God. And the peace of God, which surpasses all comprehension, will guard your hearts and your minds in Christ Jesus. (Philippians 4:6–7)

I had a breakthrough, and oh, how I needed it! In prayer I gave my fears to God as Paul said to do, and lo and behold, I got real peace in their place! There is no way to explain it; it is a work of God. I had read those verses for most of my life, and one day, when I truly needed God's peace, I found it by acting in faith on his Word. It's still working for me today.

Times of trial can be opportunities to turn to God and reach out to him as never before. Those who do, as Marj and I and so many others have done, find grace for the difficulties. In God there is strength, comfort, and his presence with us through the dark valleys.

Whenever I am hit with a new trial, I cry out to God in prayer because I know he listens to me. Then I turn to his Word in order to listen to *him*. "Has anyone else ever struggled the way I am, God?" Yes, others have suffered all kinds of trials. The Psalms are filled with such struggles! But as we read the Psalms, we come to realize they are also full of comfort, strength, and promises in response to those struggles. Through praying the Psalms, I can join in the writers' pleas to the Lord, who hears our prayers. In return, the Word of God is used by the Spirit of God to teach and comfort me as I listen to him in Scripture.

Times of trial and suffering have a way of getting our attention, causing our spiritual antenna to be tuned to the Lord, so it is especially crucial to be in his Word in these times to let our antenna receive God's truth. In it, we will find hope and peace and strength.

Today, I encourage you to sit down with the Bible and perhaps a journal or notebook. Cry out to the Lord, and then listen as you read the Word. What is he saying to you? Where is the opportunity for growth before you today? What is the new perspective his Word brings?

If you are in a time of suffering, I can guarantee God is calling you. There is no better time than now to listen for his voice in his Word.

Chapter 5

The Scriptures, Our Life

I remember well my daily struggles with fear, pain, and uncertainty in the days of cancer treatment, crying many tears as I talked to God. Though Randy was able to be with me for a few months at the beginning of my treatment, most of that year and a half he was back in West Virginia working while I stayed in California. Every day I turned to the Bible. I poured out my heart to God in prayer as I read his Word.

I once wrote on my blog:

> The Scriptures, God's words to us, sustain me daily. They are our life. They bring the only light to this dark path.

At the end of his wilderness journey, Moses knew he was about to die. He had faithfully obeyed the words of the Lord. He led the Israelites out of Egypt, bore up under the crushing load of their complaining and rebellion against God (and himself), and gave them the law of God, the first five books of the Bible.

Before he turned over the reins of leadership to Joshua, Moses sang a scathing song of warning and chastisement before giving the Israelites one last charge. He said:

> Take to your heart all the words with which I am warning you today, which you shall command your sons to observe carefully, even all the words of this law. *For it is not an idle word for you; indeed it is your life.* (Deuteronomy 32:46–47, emphasis mine)

These words about the Bible are for me as much as for the Israelites of thousands of years ago. The Scriptures are not idle words for me; they are my life. I take that statement to heart.

My sister, Sherri, was one semester into medical school when she got some bad news that plunged her into a trying, dark period of her life. She says she gave herself one day to feel sorry for herself (and she still allows herself one day for each recurrence of bad news), but only one day. Then she accepted the realities and moved on. Psalm 30 became her mantra.

> I will extol You, O Lord, for You have lifted me up . . . O Lord my God,
> I cried to You for help, and You healed me . . .
> You have kept me alive, that I would not go down to the pit.

Sing praise to the Lord, you His godly ones,
And give thanks to His holy name. (Psalm
30:1–4)

The Scriptures gave her encouragement to fight on day after day throughout those long, difficult months.

Sherri said she encourages others to find a passage of Scripture to make their own, as a lifeline to hold on to in their dark days. Those days are a great time to rest, wait on God, and think about him; a time to hold on to that Scripture lifeline and relax in God.

(By the way, Sherri pushed on through medical school during those dark months, graduated, and has been practicing medicine for several years. She presses on living life fully, resting in the Lord, in spite of the occasional bad news.)

I recall a time when I was facing major surgery. I'd been through this particular surgery once before, so I knew the pain and unpleasantness to come. As I lay on the gurney waiting to be rolled in to surgery, my mind searched for a comforting Scripture to cling to in my fear. Psalm 23 came to mind, and I grabbed hold of verse 3: "He guides me in the paths of righteousness for His name's sake." I silently quoted that over and over, gaining hope and encouragement that God would indeed bring me through this present danger and lead my life for his glory. He did bring me through, and that verse has been incorporated into many prayers I've prayed since then, both for myself and others.

My mom grasped onto Isaiah 40:31 as her promise-prayer for me when I was diagnosed with MG as a teenager and struggled for so many years with weakness. If you read that verse as my mother did, you will understand the significance of its declaration of hope, both spiritual and physical, in the face of debilitating disease. I quote it here in its powerful context:

> Do you not know? Have you not heard?
> The Everlasting God, the Lord, the Creator of the ends of the earth
> Does not become weary or tired.
> His understanding is inscrutable.
> He gives strength to the weary,
> And to him who lacks might He increases power.
> Though youths grow weary and tired,
> And vigorous young men stumble badly,
> *Yet those who wait for the Lord*
> *Will gain new strength;*
> *They will mount up with wings like eagles,*
> *They will run and not get tired,*
> *They will walk and not become weary.*
> (Isaiah 40:28–31, italics mine)

Do you have a favorite passage or a Scripture verse you have clung to in times of distress? Why do you think it was so meaningful at that time? It may be worth reviewing some of your old lifelines in times of distress!

As you spend time in the Word, ask God to show you a "lifeline" verse or passage for yourself. Memorize it. Meditate on it. Plumb its depths—or at least go as deep as you are capable of going in plumbing the infinite wisdom of God! You will find his words life-giving and renewing just like I, Sherri, my mother, and so many others have.

Chapter 6

Trusting God

*"Those who wait for the Lord
will gain new strength."*
Isaiah 40:31

When difficulties come into our lives, we immediately want to ask "Why?" or "Why me?" or "Why this?" Just as Isaiah called us to wait on (or "hope in") God, promising that our strength would be renewed, so we move ahead through the situation, trusting him and seeking his grace for each moment. As much as I want to be in control, I am not. But God is. Getting to the point of trust in God is crucial to maintaining sanity in the midst of suffering.

I remember one especially difficult juncture in my cancer treatment. I did not have enough information to feel comfortable with the direction I thought the cancer surgeon was going. In fact, I had a lot of fear, so I postponed the decision until I looked into it further, with much prayer.

When the issue was resolved, I wrote on my blog:

> And as to fear, fear will come. It is how we deal with it that is important. I went to the Lord (Philippians 4:6), recognizing the fear and anxiety rising up in me. I cried out (to God) for help, wisdom, direction, knowledge. I turned to my most trusted confidante and wise counselor, Randy, and we talked and prayed. His insights and encouragement helped me work through a very difficult situation. I sought out others I respect for their counsel, especially those who have gone through these same waters. I continued to seek sound medical advice.
>
> It is agonizing going through the trial, feeling the suffocating fear, the desperate need. But God has proven himself, once again, to be compassionate and faithful to hear our prayers. He gave the information we needed. He gave it within the time frame I asked.

I have, unfortunately, made many decisions based on fear, but when I trusted God instead, I found his Word to be true and trustworthy. When I was overcome by fear but gave my fears to God, I got God's peace in their place, just like he said I would (Philippians 4:6). In the case above, he guided me to a wise decision. This is just one example of how God answers our trust. There are so many more.

Like that of my friend Nicki. She told me she read my blog when I first posted about my cancer journey and wished she knew how I had peace in the midst of my fight with cancer. She hadn't had struggles like mine, and she realized she didn't have the trust in God that I did either.

Then Nicki went through eighteen months of pain, illness, and not knowing what was wrong with her after having two knee replacements. Following the seemingly successful surgeries, she developed knee pain and swelling, fever, and weakness of an unknown origin that turned her world upside down. She had to quit her job because she was too sick to work. She and her husband sought near and far for medical answers to her symptoms.

Nicki said those were the most difficult eighteen months of her life. But in the same breath, she told me she wouldn't trade them for anything. Why? Because through her struggles, she learned to trust God as never before. She told me that now, even though she still has her up days and down days, some with tears, she knows, like the old hymn says, it is well with her soul. She knows she will be okay with whatever may come because she has learned to rest in Christ, to trust God. He is in control.

"Whatever may come" is still the big unknown for Nicki. She faces two knee replacement replacements, and we who know and love her are all praying these surgeries will give Nicki her knees, and her life, back. But even if they don't, she has peace in her soul because she has learned the secret of trusting God "whatever may come."

Amy Carmichael, missionary to India during the early part of the last century, said:

> Trust, I have learned, means: to lean on, to place the weight of my confidence upon . . . And after this discovery, I've found many verses in the Psalms that provide great comfort when translated in this way. For instance, "I have trusted in (leaned on, placed my confidence in) your lovingkindness" (Psalm 13:5).

Lean all my weight, place all my confidence in the God who has proven himself faithful and able to do the impossible. Amy Carmichael lived that truth and spoke from the seat of one who suffered. This is what I need to do, and this is what Nicki did, especially during the hard times in life.

If we trust him, God transforms ugly, hurtful circumstances into beautiful things that lift up and encourage us and others and bring him glory. He can take our brokenness and make something beautiful of it.

Chapter 7

Perspective Is Everything

In the midst of trials, it's easy to lose perspective. Pain and suffering can cause us to look inward, and our world, as a result, contracts. Consisting of and revolving around only "me," our world becomes very small. The fact is, Me, Myself, and I can be very poor company. We all need something that can pull us up and out, beyond ourselves, because in suffering, there is real danger of sinking into the morass of self-pity. While there is room in suffering for legitimate grief and adjustment, self-pity is nothing to trifle with. It is destructive and comes from the devil, that old deceiver. It must be dealt with immediately and ruthlessly.

Oswald Chambers wrote, "No sin is worse than the sin of self-pity . . . It opens our mouths to spit out murmurings and our lives become craving spiritual sponges; there is nothing lovely or generous about them."[2]

Daily while going through cancer treatment, I set out for my thirty-minute walk. When the weather was clear I could see the mountains—not always the case in southern California—and my heart would rejoice. Having mountains, or a lake, or the ocean, or even a garden to look at refreshed my soul. I felt my spirit expand as I drank in the vista. Weights on my spirit fell away as I realized anew how big God is—bigger than those mountains—and how wonderful his world. I always talked with God as I walked.

One day I wrote in my blog:

> Just this past week I was walking . . . and talking with the Lord and asking forgiveness for and strength against self-pity. That is one thing that is so terribly damaging and destructive. I want no part of it. So I have to resist it when it raises its ugly head. I realized that I need to raise my sights and look at God's bigger world, its great needs and his heart of compassion for those who are suffering. So many are spiritually dead and need life only he can give. So many brothers and sisters in the faith are struggling and suffering terribly. I need to care more, pray more for them . . . Perspective.

During these days, the Word of God informed my thoughts and prayers. It functioned much like the views of the mountains: it lifted my eyes off myself and gave me that new, needed perspective by elevating my vision to the greater world around me, not the false world of just me and my problems.

Barbara grasped the importance of perspective when, after a two-year battle with leukemia, her faith was challenged anew by the selling of their house. She related:

> The night before last I stayed awake all night worrying about our house and selling it. I was exhausted and . . . prayed that I could take this worry about the house and completely turn it over to God . . . How come I had such a hard time trusting him?
>
> All the time I worried yesterday, God was thinking, "Oh child, I have a gift for you . . ." Last night, my doctor called me and was so excited: "Your leukemia is in remission!"
>
> My biggest gift from him was putting my worrying in perspective: the house is nothing compared to his healing me.

Even in the midst of major battles we can get mired in smaller skirmishes and must be reminded to "Trust in the Lord with all your heart and lean not on your own understanding" (Proverbs 3:5). The Word of God calls us back to trust in him, rest in him, for everything big or small.

Chapter 8

Building on the Foundation

"Therefore everyone who hears these
words of Mine and acts on them, may
be compared to a wise man . . ."
Matthew 7:24

Foundations are of great importance, but they are not the whole building. Foundations are meant to be built upon. It matters how I build my life and with what materials (1 Corinthians 3:10-15). Living in a physical world, I need to remember the spiritual realities: "It is written, 'Man shall not live on bread alone, but on every word that proceeds out of the mouth of God'" (Matthew 4:4, Deuteronomy 8:3).

Having laid a foundation in the Word of God, it makes sense to continue to build with that good material. I am convinced the Bible must hold a place of high priority in my life (2 Timothy 2:15). As I've already shared, I make time to get into the

Word, reading it, thinking about what I've read, and studying it. Then, to get it from my head to my heart and life, with God's help, I strive to put it into practice as a doer of the Word (James 1:21–25).

From my cancer blog:

> Waiting on the Lord. I am again reading through the book of Isaiah (I highly recommend it) and today read chapter 40. Wow. These passages are so amazing and powerful. They feed the soul, build one's faith. We neglect the reading and study of the Word of God to our own detriment. God had these words written down for us! I am so thankful he did that. I pray we will always be able to have the Word of God and that those who do not now have it, will be able to get it. I pray that we will eat it as food and be changed by putting into practice what God has said.

Jesus told his disciples to go into the world and make disciples (Matthew 28:19–20). That mandate applies to me, as a follower of Jesus, as well as to Peter, James, and John. I came to a point in my life when I desired with all my being to serve God, although I didn't know how that would look. But when I gave my life wholly to the Lord, I was saying I'd go anywhere and do anything to serve him, poor health and all.

God takes us at our word . . . *yes*, poor health and all! And he calls each of us in different ways to different tasks. A major step in my obedience to the Lord has been joining my husband in the call of God to sell our home and move across the country to start a ministry living among the poor in West Virginia. Following weeks of prayer and fasting, we founded Mustard Seeds and Mountains, committing ourselves to serve God through that ministry for a minimum of twenty years. After twenty-three years of striving to faithfully follow and serve the Lord, we look back and see the handprints of God all over each day, year after year, as he has faithfully led and provided for us. And the journey hasn't ended yet.

What may seem humorous to many is that it can be harder for me to walk across the road to meet a new neighbor than to pack up and move across the country to start a new work and trust God to supply for it! But that is exactly the way it is for me.

I remember my first days at college. I knew no one, and shy, introverted me made up my mind to introduce myself to the four girls sharing the room across the hall. That I could do this and did it was an epiphany for me. I actually had to talk to myself (in my head) to get myself to do it. The girls I met weren't scary and mean; they were nice and kind, and they became my friends.

I did the same thing when we moved to West Virginia. I told myself I'd go and introduce myself to each of my near neighbors. And I did. The neighbor I had the hardest time getting out to meet was the young woman I ended up having the closest relationship with.

I did these things, pushing myself out of my comfort zone, in obedience to God. I knew God wanted me to meet the people around me so I could share his love with them. You can't *always* love people from afar, especially when they live across the hall or next door!

Five months into my cancer treatment, I began chemotherapy. A month later Randy and I celebrated thirty-five years of marriage before he flew back to West Virginia. I wrote in my blog about us and our relationship to God and his Word:

> God has been our "traveling companion" all these years. Where would we be without him? We shudder to think. So how crazy would it be to look anywhere else than to him for continuing the journey? He alone has "the words of eternal life" (John 6:68) as Peter so aptly put it so very long ago.

I believe the Bible is vitally important as a foundation for our lives and as a stabilizing factor in our times of trouble. It has played a major role in my life by pointing me to the Lord, encouraging me in times of fear and uncertainty, and giving me perspective and hope in the midst of the upheaval of my circumstances. Through regular reading and study of God's Word, with the goal of putting God's truths into practice in my life, I have been able to maintain balance and wholeness mentally, emotionally, and spiritually during times of physical and emotional distress. I have experienced over and over the exchange of fear for peace: my fear for the peace of God. It is available to all who look to the Lord in faith.

At all times, but especially when we are hurting—regardless of the source of that hurt—we need that which is beyond and above ourselves and our human limitations. We need the God who spoke and still speaks today through his eternal Word. His words minister life and hope to us. This whole world will pass away, but God's Word will last forever. When we build on the foundation of his Word in obedience to him, we find ourselves gaining access to everything we could possibly need.

Part 3

Prayer

Chapter 9

Like a Child

*"Speak to Him thou for He hears,
and Spirit with Spirit can meet—
Closer is He than breathing,
and nearer than hands and feet."*
Alfred, Lord Tennyson

Prayer is as integral a part of my life as breathing. I cannot imagine not being able to pray! Prayer is communicating with God, talking to him in the ordinary days of life, crying out to him with tears in the trying times. Talking to God, honestly and humbly, like a child, is the heart of relationship with him.

One morning as my husband and I sat on our porch to pray together, we waited in silence, enjoying the beauty of the day. We are no strangers to silence; we are comfortable with it. We quiet our hearts and focus on God as we come into his presence. We do not feel we have to fill the silence with our words. When we feel like saying something to God aloud, we then speak.

That day we ended up not praying a word out loud, but we enjoyed that beautiful time in company with God, praising him for the beauty around us, communing with him in our spirits as though he was sitting on our porch swing with us—for he was with us. Jesus said, "For where two or three have gathered together in My name, I am there in their midst" (Matthew 18:20).

I like to think of God being with us like he was early on with Adam and Eve. "They heard the sound of the LORD God walking in the garden in the cool of the day" (Genesis 3:8). Many Bible commentators say the words here indicate the breeze caused by the cooling air, probably in the evening.[3] Though in this verse Adam and Eve ran and hid themselves from God because they had sinned against him, I'm sure that in prior days they had gone companionably walking and talking with God when he came into the garden to meet with them. In my imagination, I see them eager to share their day's experiences with God and hear what he had to say to them.

I love the concept of hearing the sound or voice of the LORD God walking in the garden in the cooling breeze as the sun was setting. Adam and Eve heard the familiar rustle of the leaves of the trees and bushes and knew God was coming for a chat.

The reference to the breeze or wind in Genesis 3 makes me think of two things Jesus said. He told Nicodemus, "The wind blows where it wishes and you hear the sound of it, but do not know where it comes from and where it is going; so is everyone who is born of the Spirit" (John 3:8). Shortly after that, he told the woman he met at the well in Samaria, "God is spirit, and those who worship Him must worship in spirit and truth" (John 4:24). We hear his sound in the wind: God walking in the garden, God speaking to our spirits—and "Spirit with Spirit can meet."[4]

God was with us that day as we sat quietly on the porch, hearing the wind in the trees, the birds singing, and the creek gurgling as it tumbled down the mountainside. God is present with us by his indwelling Spirit who, Jesus told his followers, will "be with you forever; that is the Spirit of truth, whom the world cannot receive, because it does not see Him or know Him, but you know Him because He abides with you and will be in you" (John 14:16–17).

I have been learning to know God for many years. In college my imagination was captured by the title of a little book by Brother Lawrence: *The Practice of the Presence of God.*[5] Although it wasn't until much later that I actually read the book, I began contemplating what it meant to practice being *conscious* of God with me. It marked the beginning of my journey of consciously living my life in his presence. We cannot see God in visible form, but he is there like he was with Adam and Eve; he is *in* those of us who have put our faith in Jesus.

When I speak of walking and talking with God, and when I affirm that he is in and with me by his Holy Spirit, I am not referring to a "buddy-buddy," overly familiar type of relationship with God—one that puts God on the level of my "pal." That is not a biblical perspective on how we should relate to God. Nowhere in Scripture will you find a person who loves God and strives to live God's way who has a flippant, cavalier attitude toward the God of the universe. Oswald Chambers wrote, "The people who are flippant and familiar are those who have never yet been introduced to Jesus Christ. After the amazing delight and liberty of realizing what Jesus Christ *does*, comes the impenetrable darkness of realizing Who He *is*."[6]

The Scriptures refer to God as loving, listening to, and blessing those who fear the Lord (Psalm 31:19), who hold him in reverence and seek to live by his Word. He is and always will be God—holy— "other" than us. He is Creator, we are his creation. We must always approach him in humility and with reverential fear. The prophet Micah put it well: "He has told you, O man, what is good; and what does the LORD require of you but to do justice, to love kindness, and to walk humbly with your God?" (Micah 6:8).

We approach God in prayer with humility and live before him in the same humility. Pride can't coexist with humility or with God! Jesus made this very clear when he was asked who was greatest in the kingdom of heaven. He placed a child in the midst of those he was teaching and said, "Truly I say to you, unless you are converted and become like children, you will not enter the kingdom of heaven. Whoever then humbles himself as this child, he is the greatest in the kingdom of heaven" (Matthew 18:3–4).

In Matthew 11:25, Jesus thanked his Father for revealing his truths to children, not the wise and learned of the world. The truths of God are made known to those who have faith in and walk humbly with him like a child—in trials, in suffering, in good times, and in the cool of the day.

Chapter 10

Types of Prayer

In the Bible and in prayer, God talks with us, revealing his truths, and we respond. But who started the conversation?

God.

God has been initiating communication with mankind since he first created us. He blessed Adam and Eve, our first parents, telling them to have children and populate the earth. He gave them meaningful work, instructing them to be the overseers and caretakers of his creation, in fact, to rule over it; and he gave them the authority and provision to carry out that task (Genesis 1:27–30). In those days when the wind in the trees announced his arrival, God was involved in their daily lives. He desired Adam and Eve's companionship, and he desires ours as well (Psalm 18:19, Psalm 105:43).

God initiated communication with us. He wants us to reciprocate. One way we do that is through prayer, in its many different forms.

In the simplest terms, prayer is talking to God. Though there are many different kinds of prayer, and this is by no means a treatise on the subject, I will touch on two different types of prayer that are especially relevant for those in times of brokenness: intercession and personal petition.[7]

Intercession

> Thank you many times over for your prayers of faith for me and Randy. Please don't give up!

Intercession is praying for another person or group of people. It is coming to God on behalf of another. Jesus, as our Great High Priest in heaven, has the ministry of intercession for us now. He stands before our heavenly Father, speaks on our behalf, and advocates for us (1 Timothy 2:5; Hebrews 4:14, 15; Hebrews 7:24, 25; 1 John 2:1). He is our perfect Advocate, like the very best courtroom lawyer. He lived here on Earth as a human and understands us perfectly, and because he always pleads for us according to God's will, he is always heard (Hebrews 4:14–16; Hebrews 5:7–10).

The Spirit of God, who lives in those of us who trust Jesus for salvation, intercedes for us as well with groans that cannot be put into words (Romans 8:26). And of course, his intercession for us is done perfectly and according to the will of God because the Spirit of God knows what the will of God is (Romans 8:27).

We, too, are told to intercede for others, praying to God on their behalf (1 Timothy 2:1–4; Ephesians 6:18–19).

In my mind, I picture intercession this way: When I intercede for a friend, I step between my friend and God and plead her cause like a trial lawyer would do for his client before the judge. Of course, because my understanding is finite, I must seek out the mind and will of God in the whole process. In this case, the Judge is for us! God's knowledge is infinite; he knows what is best for my friend. Since my knowledge is limited, I am just guessing unless I ask the Lord for insight in how to pray for the very best outcome. Even in my uncertainty of how to pray, as I continue to seek God's mind, I have the certainty that he will answer according to his will, for my friend's good and God's glory.

Amy Carmichael said of prayer, "It is a petty view of our Father's love and wisdom which demands or expects an answer according to our desires apart from His wisdom."[8] Without seeking God's mind and will for prayer, we flounder in the task of intercession. The purpose of prayer is to get to know God and join him in doing his will on earth. It's not what we want but what he wants. When we pray according to God's will, we pray with power—the very power of God.

Boosted by Prayers

When others pray for your needs, they are interceding for you. When people pray for me, I can't help but feel on the one hand how humbling it is, and yet, on the other hand, how important it is that they continue! How desperately needed and deeply appreciated are the prayers of others when we are going through difficult times!

As I wrote in my blog during cancer treatment:

> Another "booster shot" of encouragement for me is to know you all are praying for me. I cannot tell you enough how important that is to me. I believe in the community of the saints. There is power when we come together before his throne of grace to receive mercy and find grace to help us in our time of need. I still believe that "man's extremity is God's opportunity."[9] What is hopeless and impossible with us is not so for God, for all things are possible with God.
>
> I remember, when I was just a teenager lying in a hospital bed, learning that my church family and the church families of other relatives were praying for me, even though most of them had never met me. To hear that people, even people I didn't know and who didn't know me, were praying for me was an eye-opening experience. Though I had attended church prayer meetings much of my life, this was a new experience in the world of prayer.
>
> I cannot even put into words the impact it has had on me, and not just because God answered so many prayers on my behalf.

This was schooling in prayer I might not have realized any other way. It has changed my view and appreciation of prayer in a powerful way, this knowing that other people were praying for me, day after day.

It was also schooling in the caring, family aspect of the church. People who had not met her cared enough for a young girl to pray for her. That girl was me, and I felt deeply thankful.

Today people all over the country pray for me, and I am humbled and grateful beyond words. I am encouraged by them to love others the same way, praying for them in their need.

The intercessory prayers of others are very important. As I went through months of cancer treatment, intercession became an important reality for me once again:

I realized this morning that I am under more stress than I was aware. As Randy said recently, I've gone through a lot over the past eighteen months: the diagnosis of my breast cancer in December, decisions of where to get treatment, fear of cancer and fear of how I would tolerate treatments because of the weakness of MG; changing residences from West Virginia to California and living in others' homes, going through two surgeries, two chemotherapy regimens, losing my hair and slowly gaining it back, radiation and ongoing Herceptin infusions, and everything else medical with it; months of separation from Randy; the joys of being with children and grandchildren, and even new friends and ministry in the local church. Now I've had the brakes put on suddenly and must shift gears to prepare myself for leaving all this to go back and resume my life in West Virginia. It is taking an emotional toll . . . *I appreciate so much your prayers for me, even when you may not know what I need at any given time; God does know.*

During more recent crises in my life, people have again prayed for me. All these prayers over all these years have powerfully affected my life in more ways than just physical healing, and I will be eternally thankful.

For those of us in trials and suffering, the reality of intercession raises questions. Do prayers really affect outcomes? We wouldn't pray if we didn't believe they did. From the testimony of Scripture and my own personal experience, I can say with absolute certainty, yes, prayers make a difference. I wholeheartedly agree with the apostle James:

Confess your sins to one another, and pray for one another so that you may be healed. The effective prayer of a righteous man can accomplish much. Elijah was a man with a nature like ours, and he prayed earnestly that it would not rain, and it did not rain on the earth for three years and six months. Then he prayed again, and the sky poured rain and the earth produced its fruit. (James 5:16–18)

When I moved in with my son and his family to start down the long road of cancer treatment, one of the first things Randy and I did was contact the pastor of the church our sons attended. We asked the leaders to anoint me with oil and pray for my healing from cancer and MG, as James says to do. They did that and continued to pray for me during my time there. The caring people of that church became my church family.

Eleven months into cancer treatment, God answered our prayers for healing from the severe weakness of MG. Though initially I had feared surgery and the possible negative side effects of chemotherapy and radiation, I sailed through my two surgeries, was only sick about one time in two sets of chemo, and had no negative side effects from radiation. Two years after the start of cancer treatment I was declared cancer free and remain so to this day.

Does prayer affect outcomes? I believe it does. I believe God acted in answer to prayer.

When we take the time to pray and seek the mind of God, prayers do have effect. We may not always understand what God is doing, but he can be relied on to do the right thing.

Personal Petition

Prayer is weakness leaning on omnipotence. (W.S. Bowd)

As I drove away from the doctor's office yesterday I felt like crying. And I did a little. I had just been to the cardiologist, who gave me the results of three heart tests I had done two weeks ago. I already knew I have irregular heartbeats and was put on . . . medication, but the tests also showed my heart is weak and functioning at 35% (ejection fraction) rather than a much higher percentage. So I felt my throat tighten up and I silently cried out to the Lord as I drove away . . .

My cardiologist said she doesn't know if the weakening of my heart is related to the chemotherapy I received (there are two drugs which I did receive that can cause heart problems). Before my cancer surgery last February I had heart tests done and they came back normal. My current test results are being sent to my oncologist . . .

I am not overburdened with this news but I am saddened . . . I think it is similar to what the psalmist may have felt sometimes when he would say, "How long, Lord?" I really can't describe my feelings. *I only know how I respond to my feelings, and that is to cry out to God, who hears.* Sometimes I don't even have words; I don't even know what I am feeling to be able to form words. But that is okay, because he listens to my heart. I don't need words. He gives me peace. *I am praying* and asking God to heal me of these conditions, strengthen my heart and regulate the beats.

Somewhat different from intercessory prayer, which focuses on praying for others, is prayer for our own selves, asking God about things that are dear to our hearts or for needs sorely felt. How often I have cried out to God for myself!

In the play *Shadowlands*, the story of the life of writer C.S. Lewis, he is quoted as saying, "I pray because I can't help myself. I pray because I'm helpless. I pray because the need flows out of me all the time—waking and sleeping. It does not change God—it changes me."[10]

I regularly read the Psalms, and from them I have learned much about praying for myself. In fact, I often personalize a psalm as I read it, making it my own prayer. The psalmists, who lived in a brutal world of warriors and conquerors, spoke about human enemies. I live in a peaceful setting, but I know I have an enemy of my soul, and he wishes to destroy me. The apostle Peter tells us that our "adversary, the devil, prowls around like a roaring lion, seeking someone to devour" (1 Peter 5:8). So when the psalmist cries out to God against his enemy, I think of my archenemy, the devil, and I make the psalmist's prayer my own.

Psalm 64 comes closest to an accurate prayer for a situation we might face today. Though King David had enemies who fought against him with swords and arrows, he also had enemies whose weapons were their evil tongues as they conspired against him. Can you relate to someone who says hurtful and damaging things about you or others? That sort of enemy is perfectly depicted in this psalm. If we find ourselves in a similar situation, we can make David's prayer our own. See how he poured out his heart to God and then note how his trust was rewarded:

> Lord, listen to my complaint: Oh, preserve my life from the conspiracy of these wicked men, these gangs of criminals. They cut me down with sharpened tongues; they aim their bitter words like arrows straight at my heart. They shoot from ambush at the innocent. Suddenly the deed is done, yet they are not afraid. They encourage each other to do evil. They meet in secret to set their traps. "He will never notice them here," they say. They keep a sharp lookout for opportunities of crime. They spend long hours with all their endless evil thoughts and plans.
>
> But God himself will shoot them down. Suddenly his arrow will pierce them. They will stagger backward, destroyed by those they spoke against. All who see it happening will scoff at them. (Psalm 64:1-8, TLB)

The Lord works on our behalf in answer to our prayers, but notice the other outcome the psalmist points out:

> Then everyone shall stand in awe and confess the greatness of the miracles of God; at last they will realize what amazing things he does. And the godly shall rejoice in the Lord, and trust and praise him. (Psalm 64:9-10, TLB)

The psalms teach us that there is more going on in our personal struggles than meets the eye. We will delve into that in later chapters. For now, it is encouraging to realize that when we pray as the psalmists did, we join a great company of the faithful who have proven that trusting God makes good sense and gets results.

Jonah prayed prayers inside the belly of the fish that sounded much like the psalms he surely was familiar with. God obviously heard him, for the fish had a Jonah-sized bellyache and spit him out. Priscilla Shirer, in her book *Jonah: Navigating a Life Interrupted,* says, "No prayer is more effective than the one that finds its roots in the pages of God's Word."[11]

Like Jonah, I know what it means to cry out to God knowing that if he doesn't answer and spare my life, I truly will not survive. In the first chapter of this book I told about a crisis situation in a hospital when I began to choke; I was literally choking to death. My silent prayers echoed drowning Peter's cries: "Lord, save me!" I knew that if God didn't act on my behalf, I was going to die.

> Blessed be the Lord, because He has heard the voice of my supplication. The Lord is my strength and my shield; my heart trusts in Him, and I am helped; Therefore my heart exults, and with my song I shall thank Him. (Psalm 28:6–7)

> Blessed be the Lord, who daily bears our burden, the God who is our salvation. Selah. God is to us a God of deliverances; and to God the Lord belong escapes from death. (Psalm 68:19–20)

Not every prayer I've prayed has been answered in the way I have desired, but God has graciously heard me and others on my behalf so many times I could never count them. My response is overwhelming gratitude and praise to God.

Part 1 of this book focused on the importance of making the Bible central to our lives. It's worth reiterating here how much the Bible and prayer go hand in hand. Prayer is an act of faith, and my faith in God is strengthened as I look at who he is. I do that by turning to the Bible. Along with reading other books of the Bible, I daily read a psalm to learn more about the Person of God and his great works and to tune my heart to enter into praise.

I have often "camped out" in a section of Scripture rather than just passing by it with a once-over reading. This can be a tremendous source of prayer. I have looked closely at a psalm or other passage of Scripture, spent some time there, and come back to it later to think and feel my way through the words. Psalm 33, for example, is like a treasure box jam-packed with nuggets about God, communicated in a dramatic and poetic way. Entering into these words lifts my spirit, letting me see things from a higher perspective, drawing me close into God. Praying psalms like this one is especially beneficial in times of trial.

> Let the godly sing for joy to the Lord; it is *fitting* for the pure to praise him . . . and sing with joy. *For the word of the Lord holds true, and we can trust everything he does.* He loves whatever is just and good; the *unfailing love of the Lord fills the earth.*
>
> *The Lord merely spoke, and the heavens were created* . . . Let the whole world fear the Lord, and let everyone stand in awe of him.
>
> *The Lord's plans stand firm forever; his intentions can never be shaken.*
>
> The Lord looks down from heaven and sees the whole human race. From his throne he observes all who live on the earth. He made their hearts, so he understands everything they do.
>
> *The Lord watches over those who fear him, those who rely on his unfailing love. He rescues them from death and keeps them alive in times of famine.*

> We put our hope in the Lord. *He is our help and our shield. In him our hearts rejoice, for we trust in his holy name.*
>
> *Let your unfailing love surround us, Lord,* for our hope is in you alone.
>
> (Psalm 33, selected verses, NLT, emphasis mine)

What a treasure trove of wonderful truths! As I read, my faith in God is built up even as I pour out my heart to him. I can be real with God, for he has always been real with me. I can entrust myself to God and be encouraged because of who he is: holy, trustworthy, loving, never failing, all powerful. He knows me, he is in control and has a plan, and he knows where he wants to take me. He is my help.

There are many types of prayer, with intercession and personal petition being two of the most commonly known and practiced. The point of both is to come before God and seek his will so we can pray with great effectiveness, like Elijah did. When we take a chance on God and fully trust in him, we find, like Jonah and the psalmists did, that he is our Deliverer. He is the God who answers prayer.

> *"Trust in Him at all times, O people;*
> *pour out your heart before Him;*
> *God is a refuge for us."*
> Psalm 62:8

Chapter 11

Prayer: Just Do It . . .
But How?

Lord, I'm at the same old place again. I just can't do this. These people and their needs have to be in my heart when I pray for them, not just words on my prayer list where I tick them off one by one. That's not praying. Help me, Lord!

I distinctly remember when, as a college student, I cried out this way in frustration to God. My "prayer life" wasn't working. I would make my prayer list and start my prayers by asking God this and that for so-and-so, and I meant it wholeheartedly. This would last for a day or two, but time after time my fervor would dwindle into mechanical words read from a list. I knew I had to pray with my heart, but I didn't know how to maintain the transfer from my head to my heart. I sincerely yearned to communicate with

God and effect change through prayer on behalf of others in need, yet I usually ended up feeling that I was falling short. I didn't know what to do about it, so I did the only thing I *did* know to do: I asked God to help me.

A few years later I was introduced to a simple way of entering into God's presence in prayer, one that's easy to remember and rooted in the Scriptures. It changed the way I prayed and as a result, changed my life. It is called the ACTS of prayer.[12]

The acrostic stands for:

Adoration. Approach God in humility, reverence, and awe, and worship him for who he is. We learn about him as we read and study the Bible. He is holy, and we must approach him as such (Luke 11:2).

Confession. Sin acts as a wall between us and God, effectively blocking our prayers (Isaiah 59:2). We need to be sensitive to God's Spirit on a daily basis as he speaks conviction to us, confessing and repenting of all known sin as soon as we are aware of it. That way, communication with God remains open (1 John 1:8–9).

Thanksgiving. The greatest acceptable sacrifice we can make to God (besides laying our lives at his feet as a living sacrifice, as Paul tells us to do in Romans 12:1) is the sacrifice of thanksgiving and praise (Hebrews 13:15). Our prayers are to be seasoned with gratitude.

Supplication. This is the part we normally think of as prayer: asking God for something (Luke 11:9–10). Our requests must be couched in the reverence and worship due God as we seek first his will in the matter, with our heart purged of known sin through confession and repentance, wrapped in trust, and infused with thanksgiving.

Perhaps the disciples had difficulties and frustrations in prayer similar to mine, for they asked Jesus to teach them to pray:

> It happened that while Jesus was praying in a certain place, after He had finished, one of His disciples said to Him, "Lord, teach us to pray just as John also taught his disciples."
>
> And He said to them, "When you pray, say: 'Father, hallowed be Your name.
>
> Your kingdom come.
>
> Give us each day our daily bread.
>
> And forgive us our sins,
>
> For we ourselves also forgive everyone who is indebted to us.
>
> And lead us not into temptation.'" (Luke 11:1–4)

Jesus taught his disciples to enter God's presence by first honoring and worshiping him. Approaching God by focusing my attention on him, worshiping and adoring him, gave me a whole new perspective on prayer, and on my whole Christian life. I began to live more and more with my eyes toward God, rather than on me and my needs or even others' needs.

This progression of understanding didn't happen all at once but grew over the years. (God is so patient!) Confession of sin and thanksgiving naturally flow from putting our eyes on Jesus. How can it not be so? Then our hearts are in a better state—more humble and tender—to enter into supplication, which is asking God to do something about the need at hand.

There are, of course, times when all we can do is burst out, "Lord help me!" But my usual way is to come to God in prayer by first focusing on him, then moving to the other elements.

There are other biblical prayers we can learn from. These forms are only means to an end. Prayer—just do it!

Chapter 12

Prayer as Relationship

"Pray then like this: 'Our Father in heaven . . .'"
Matthew 6:9

Prayer is not about conjuring and magic. It is not about coercing God or persuading him to do something we ask. Prayer is about relationship with our heavenly Father, the Everlasting God (Matthew 6:9). He is the God who is Lord and Master over all. He is sovereign. He has the final say, not us. He knows what he has planned for us and others and what will be best for us in the greater scheme of things, because he does have a greater scheme of things! He acts out of who he is, for our good and to accomplish his greater purposes. In prayer we seek his mind, his will, for how to pray about things and people.

Oswald Chambers said:

> Worship and intercession must go together,
> the one is impossible without the other.
> Intercession means we rouse ourselves up to
> get the mind of Christ about the one for whom
> we pray. Too often instead of worshipping God,
> we construct statements as to how prayer
> works . . . We hurl our own petitions at God's
> throne and dictate to Him as to what we wish
> Him to do. We do not worship God, nor do we
> seek the mind of Christ.[13]

Boy, that hit home with me! How often I have prayed that way, hurling my petitions at God, telling him what I think is best, trying to convince him to see things my way, mentally trying to work out the solution to the problem I'm asking God about. I wasn't seeking the mind and will of God; I was trying to convince God of my will. Thankfully, God has been patiently teaching me to pray over the years. I'm still learning.

Prayer is about relationship, relationship with God. Prayer is not about demanding from God what I want, telling him when and how to answer my prayers; it is about finding out what God wants to accomplish. What Chambers said about intercession holds true for prayer for ourselves as well. We must seek his mind, his purposes, as Christ did in the garden of Gethsemane.

Mark Galli wrote that the great purpose of God is "nothing less than the salvation of humankind . . . in a rehabilitated earth." He goes on to say:

> Prayer and the unchanging purpose of God embrace in two ways. First and foremost, in prayer we align ourselves with the unchanging will of God; we learn to swim with the current and not against it; we learn to say, "Not my will, but thine be done."[14]

In prayer we come to God, laying our desires before him honestly and openly, at the same time willing to bow to God's will should our will not align with his. In the garden of Gethsemane, Jesus brought his heavyhearted desire to his Father and honestly asked him to remove the crushing burden of what was to come. And yet Jesus, who was God in human flesh, ultimately came to the place of submission because in communicating with his Father, he came to understand the mind and purposes of God. For Jesus, God's purposes superseded personal will. God the Father's will became the will of Jesus the Son. Grasping this in our own lives is of utmost importance in our understanding and practice of prayer.

Jesus told his disciples that "the Helper, the Holy Spirit, whom the Father will send in My name, He will teach you all things, and bring to your remembrance all that I have said to you" (John 14:26, ESV). As we study the Bible, as we practice God's presence, as we seek to understand God's will generally and specifically, we are informed by God's Spirit of his will so that as we wrestle in prayer we are reminded by his Spirit of his desires, plans, and purposes.

The question then becomes, do I go confidently to God, willing to argue my point yet truthfully seeking to align my will with the will of God? Or is "Thy will be done" just a phrase tacked on to my prayer, devoid of meaning? We must choose the best way and be convinced that God's way *is* the best way, regardless of how scary or difficult it may appear. We must trust God at this point.

> Good and upright is the Lord. (Psalm 25:8, NIV)

> Oh, taste and see that the Lord is good; blessed is the man who trusts in Him! (Psalm 34:8, NKJV)

> Trust in the Lord and do good. (Psalm 37:3, NKJV)

Our faith in God is not just in what he can do, but in himself, in who he is. What God does comes out of who he is. This is where our faith must take root—believing that God is who he says he is and that he is working for our best and his glory.

Trusting God may be especially hard, yet especially crucial, when we are in pain or fear because of circumstances beyond our control.

> O Lord God, you are God, and your words are true. (2 Samuel 7:28, ESV)

Not to us, O Lord, not to us, but to Your name give glory because of Your lovingkindness, because of Your truth. (Psalm 115:1)

For the word of the Lord holds true, and we can trust everything he does. (Psalm 33:4, NLT)

Trust in God must be cultivated. It must become the bedrock from which we pray. Desiring God himself and his way should be more important to us than desiring only what he can do for us. This truth has helped me immeasurably as I have cried out to him in pain or fear or simply not knowing which way to turn. As the keel of a boat keeps it upright and moving forward when it is buffeted by severe weather, so keeping my vision fixed on the character and purposes and will of God, who is compassionate and gracious (Exodus 34:6), keeps me stable and moving in the right direction when I'm buffeted about by great waves of pain, fear, and the looming unknown.

Chapter 13

Prayer as Our Lifeline

"Let us learn to think of tears as liquid prayers."
Charles Spurgeon

Prayer is our lifeline, our direct line of communication with God the Father. We cry out to God when we are in need and when we are hurting, whatever form that hurt may take. My suffering, for the most part, has been physical. Others have experienced rejection, abuse, the loss of a loved one, economic uncertainty, persecution for their faith in Jesus Christ, or fill-in-the-blank. It seems there is no limit to the forms pain can take. Yet, regardless of the trial, God is a compassionate and gracious God, a God who is "abounding in lovingkindness" (Exodus 34:6), and he acts in mercy and grace toward us, hearing us when we cry out to him, for he is the God "who hears prayer," the One to whom "all men come" (Psalm 65:2). We can gain great comfort and confidence from this; comfort for our hurting hearts and confidence to come before him because we are learning, in the midst of our trials, how good and loving and kind he is.

> Bless the Lord, O my soul, and all that is within me, bless His holy name. Bless the Lord, O my soul, and forget none of His benefits; who pardons all your iniquities, who heals all your diseases; who redeems your life from the pit, who crowns you with lovingkindness and compassion; who satisfies your years with good things, so that your youth is renewed like the eagle. (Psalm 103:1–5)

During my cancer treatment, many times—daily—I cried out to God. Pain especially makes me vulnerable to tears. Fear has a similar effect. My default response is to pray, talking and often crying with tears to God. To this day, I work hard at holding it together emotionally in public, but in private, just me and God, I hold back nothing from him. I know I can unload my fears, my uncertainties, my anxieties, my tears on him, and he will understand. He can take it. We are always accepted by him, never rejected. We can be vulnerable and open with the Lord, for no one who comes to him in that way is ever rejected.

I also know God is the only one who can really do anything about my hurts and fears. Having a friend or loved one's shoulder to cry on, someone to hold our hand in the hard times, is immeasurably valuable, and I in no way want to diminish how important it is. But the truth is, we dare not lean too heavily on any person. There is only One who can bear, and has borne, our sorrows, our pains: Jesus.

> For we do not have a High Priest who cannot sympathize with our weaknesses, but was in all points tempted as we are, yet without sin. Let us therefore come boldly to the throne of grace, that we may obtain mercy and find grace to help in time of need. (Hebrews 4:15–16, NKJV)

I take that invitation literally. I lean hard on Jesus! He has never collapsed in fatigue. He has never failed to keep holding me together. He can and does work to change what I cannot change.

I've mentioned how fear has at times caused me to cry out to God. Pain, fear, and distress of all kinds creates in us the need to reach out for relief from the burden we bear. It did for Randy. He sat in a patio chair in our son's backyard, my recent cancer diagnosis fresh and painful to him, like a raw wound. He poured out his heart to God, not knowing if I would live through this battle with cancer. As he prayed, he clearly sensed God telling him, "She will not suffer." Peace descended on him from that moment.

Though he knew I'd have to go through pain and the difficult physical trials of surgeries, chemotherapy, and radiation in the process of cancer treatment, Randy also had the assurance that God would mercifully bring me through, every step of the way.

And that is exactly how I experienced it. Treatment for cancer was not pleasant nor pain free, but I did not suffer as I might have. God abundantly answered prayer, for me and for Randy.

Seven years earlier I had a similar experience while praying for my sister after we learned of her bad news. I was walking on my treadmill, crying my eyes out praying for her. As I poured out my heart to God for my sister, an overwhelming sense came over me that he would take care of her. Peace flooded me. I knew she would be okay; I didn't have to keep pleading with God for her. God is so kind and good.

God doesn't always answer with these kinds of assurances. He did not see fit to heal my dad of cancer. Our comfort in those days of extreme struggle was in knowing Dad had put his faith in Christ and had the hope of eternal life. This is our greatest comfort.

The reason we come to God is the promise we have from him that we will find mercy and grace to help in our time of need (Hebrews 4:16). When we give our anxieties (and keep on giving them) over to the Lord, he does give us peace in the midst of our unrest. Mercy, grace, and peace from God. No drug can give that! But God, in answer to prayer, can and does.

Chapter 14

Orientation for Prayer

S o far, as we've considered prayer, we've looked at types of prayer, its purposes and the way it connects us with God, especially during hard times. There are such things, however, as selfish prayers, things we ask for out of our own selfish desires with no thought of God's will. James says it loud and clear:

> What is causing the quarrels and fights among you? Don't they come from the evil desires at war within you? You want what you don't have, so you scheme and kill to get it. You are jealous of what others have, but you can't get it, so you fight and wage war to take it away from them. Yet you don't have what you want because you don't ask God for it. And even when you ask, you don't get it because your motives are all wrong—you want only what will give you pleasure. (James 4:1–3, NLT)

God is not bound by anything in Scripture to answer those kinds of prayers. No, when Jesus said "ask what you will and I'll do it," he did not mean God would answer the selfish prayers James is referring to. Jesus is clear about how and why he answers whatever we ask in his name: "*so that* the Father may be glorified in the Son" (John 14:13, emphasis mine). I always pay attention to the "so that."

In all our praying, and in fact in our everyday living, we must lay down at God's feet everything that is most precious to us, letting go of things and people—and our very own lives—submitting ourselves and what we love to the will of God. As Jesus said, we must completely desire and seek his will over our own:

> Then He said to them all, "If anyone desires to come after Me, let him deny himself, and take up his cross daily, and follow Me. For whoever desires to save his life will lose it, but whoever loses his life for My sake will save it. For what profit is it to a man if he gains the whole world, and is himself destroyed or lost?" (Luke 9:23–25, NKJV)

And:

> *If you abide in Me, and My words abide in you,* you will ask what you desire, and it shall be done for you. By this My Father is glorified, that you bear much fruit; so you will be My disciples. As the Father loved Me,

I also have loved you; abide in My love. *If*
you keep My commandments, you will abide
in My love, just as I have kept My Father's
commandments and abide in His love . . .
This is My commandment, that you *love one*
another as I have loved you. (John 15:7–10,
12, NKJV, emphasis mine)

When we come to the point of choosing God's will,
desiring what he desires and practicing a lifestyle of
obedience to the Lord, our prayers in faith will be
honored by him because our hearts will be right
with him, not in rebellion against him (John 15:7).

Prayer is about relationship. The more we get to
know God, the more we realize he can be trusted,
though our suffering and difficulties may not get
easier. When we keep on praying, the path to God's
throne of grace will become familiar territory; we
will not hesitate to take that path, for we know we
will receive a warm reception at his throne.

Prayer is vital to our lives, as important as
breathing, for it is our main avenue of communication
with God. He gives his Spirit to those of us who
put our faith in Jesus Christ for salvation. He will
be with us, guide us, and instruct us. The Spirit
intercedes for us, as does Jesus, who is our great
High Priest, standing in the presence of God the
Father on our behalf. We too have been given this
work of intercession for others, bringing them before
the Lord and pleading their case, seeking the will
of God to be done in their lives. Similarly, we pray
for ourselves, submitting our will to his because as

our Creator and loving heavenly Father, he knows what is best for us.

Prayer is about relationship with God. The more we understand his character and will, through reading the Scriptures and putting them into practice, the more we can trust him and experience his kind deeds done for us and others.

Prayer does make a difference. In every stage of life, we need to learn to effectively pray. It is not difficult; the Scriptures teach us how. God awaits us at his throne of grace, ready to help us in our time of need.

Chapter 15

Striking Back

It was during my struggle with cancer that I became aware of an aspect of prayer we've looked at just briefly, that of declaring war on my enemy, "the devil, who walks about like a roaring lion, seeking whom he may devour" (1 Peter 5:8, NKJV). War is neither nice nor desirable. But there is a place for it. As I went through treatment, I declared war on my enemy, the devil, and so did others by their prayers as they interceded for me.

Scripture teaches that "our struggle is not against flesh and blood, but against the rulers, against the powers, against the world forces of this darkness, against the spiritual forces of wickedness in the heavenly places" (Ephesians 6:12). There are spiritual, unseen powers of evil behind things that happen in this life, even those carried out by other people. Understanding the reality of evil helps make sense of Jesus's command to "love your enemies and pray for those who persecute you" (Matthew 5:44). It is not people who are our real enemies.

In this war against spiritual powers at work behind the scenes, we show no mercy and take no prisoners. In my mind, the battle is not just about me. Though I am being accused before the throne of God by Satan, the accuser of the brethren, this is also about the reputation, the renown, and the glory of the King (Job 1:6, Revelation 12:9–10). Every attack against God's creation is an attack by Satan against the Person of God.

It's revealing to look anew at the origins of evil in our world:

> The serpent was the craftiest of all the creatures the Lord God had made. So the serpent came to the woman. "Really?" he asked. "None of the fruit in the garden? God says you mustn't eat any of it?"
>
> "Of course we may eat it," the woman told him. "It's only the fruit from the tree at the center of the garden that we are not to eat. God says we mustn't eat it or even touch it, or we will die."
>
> "That's a lie!" the serpent hissed. "You'll not die! God knows very well that the instant you eat it you will become like him, for your eyes will be opened—you will be able to distinguish good from evil!"
>
> The woman was convinced. How lovely and fresh looking it was! And it would make her so wise! So she ate some of the fruit and gave

some to her husband, and he ate it too. And as they ate it, suddenly they became aware of their nakedness, and were embarrassed. So they strung fig leaves together to cover themselves around the hips.

That evening they heard the sound of the Lord God walking in the garden; and they hid themselves among the trees. The Lord God called to Adam, "Why are you hiding?"

And Adam replied, "I heard you coming and didn't want you to see me naked. So I hid."

"Who told you you were naked?" the Lord God asked. "Have you eaten fruit from the tree I warned you about?"

"Yes," Adam admitted, "but it was the woman you gave me who brought me some, and I ate it."

Then the Lord God asked the woman, "How could you do such a thing?"

"The serpent tricked me," she replied.

So the Lord God said to the serpent, "This is your punishment: You are singled out from among all the domestic and wild animals of the whole earth—to be cursed. You shall grovel in the dust as long as you live, crawling along on your belly. From now on you and the woman will be enemies, as will your offspring and hers. You will strike his heel, but he will crush your head."

Then God said to the woman, "You shall bear children in intense pain and suffering;

yet even so, you shall welcome your husband's affections, and he shall be your master."

And to Adam, God said, "Because you listened to your wife and ate the fruit when I told you not to, I have placed a curse upon the soil. All your life you will struggle to extract a living from it. It will grow thorns and thistles for you, and you shall eat its grasses. All your life you will sweat to master it, until your dying day. Then you will return to the ground from which you came. For you were made from the ground, and to the ground you will return." (Genesis 3:1–19, TLB)

When Eve was deceived into abandoning her trust in God, believing the lies of the serpent rather than God's words, the consequences were devastating. Add to that Adam's choice to side with his wife against God, and all the suffering in the world has flowed out of that decision. Now we suffer because we live in a sinful, fallen world—one that began with a serpent, a handful of lies, and a broken relationship.

Suffering of various sorts can come because we are being accused before God by Satan, who wants to discredit God. In many cases we fall into his trap, just as Eve and Adam did in the garden. Satan is happy if he can get us to doubt and disbelieve God, because then we will discredit God by our complaints and railings against him. This is what the Israelites did after God delivered them from slavery in Egypt, and this is what all too often happens when hard things happen in our lives. The first person we tend to blame is God. Rather, we need to step back and remember that the one who is accusing and attacking us is not God but Satan.

Though we may not be aware of it, God has a greater overarching plan. He is going to put down and do away with all evil, and he will reign supreme eternally. In the meantime, we stand against our enemy. Prayer is central to this stand.

We don't come against superpowers of wickedness in our puny human strength. "The weapons we fight with are not the weapons of the world. On the contrary, they have divine power to demolish strongholds" (2 Corinthians 10:4). The power that raised Jesus from the dead has been made available to us (Ephesians 1:19–20), so when we pray in the authority of the name of Jesus, God is at work through us. When we ask anything that accords with God's will, we have that for which we ask:

> And whatever you ask in My name, that I will do, that the Father may be glorified in the Son. (John 14:13)

> My little children, let us not love in word or in tongue, but in deed and in truth . . . And whatever we ask we receive from Him, because we keep His commandments and do those things that are pleasing in His sight. And this is His commandment: that we should believe on the name of His Son Jesus Christ and love one another, as He gave us commandment. (1 John 3:18, 22–23)

What does it look like to "strike back" at our enemy, Satan, especially in the midst of our trials? Randy and I took one step of faith to strike back when we went to the leaders of the church we attended, reaching out to them to include the church in my struggles against cancer. We asked them to anoint me with oil in the name of the Lord and pray for my healing from cancer and MG, which they did. Then, just like those who had prayed for my healing from MG from the time of my diagnosis when I was a teenager, we had to continue praying in faith through the months that I went through cancer treatment. Were those steps of faith worth it? Is there value in broadening the circle of prayer by going to the church to join us in prayer? Does it matter that we pray and pray?

In the next chapter I'll let you in on a not-so-secret secret about prayer that I have seen to be life-changing.

Chapter 16

Persistent Prayer

"Continue steadfastly in prayer."
Colossians 4:2

What do we do when we've prayed and prayed but God hasn't answered our prayer? One of the things God put his finger on in my life as I was going through cancer treatment had to do with persistent prayer. Jesus said we need to keep on praying, coming back over and over again, not letting go of God (Luke 18:1ff). I had been lax, letting go to an extent of prayer for my own healing from MG, the muscle weakness I've lived with since childhood.

When God showed me this, I began to pray for my healing from MG more persistently while also praying for healing from cancer. Randy boldly led the way in this, and I followed.

I think most of the time I want things so quickly that I figure if God doesn't answer right away (preferably yesterday), he is not going to answer. Wrong! My time schedules are not the same as God's, and I have to realize that I must bow to his. He knows infinitely more about me and my situation than I do and is working for my benefit even when I am unaware of it.

God is gracious and compassionate and hears the prayers of his children, unlike the unjust judge in Jesus's parable. He only grudgingly gave in after being worn down by the persistent widow who demanded justice. Listen:

> One day Jesus told his disciples a story to illustrate their need for constant prayer and to show them that they must keep praying until the answer comes.
>
> "There was a city judge," he said, "a very godless man who had great contempt for everyone. A widow of that city came to him frequently to appeal for justice against a man who had harmed her. The judge ignored her for a while, but eventually she got on his nerves.
>
> "'I fear neither God nor man,' he said to himself, 'but this woman bothers me. I'm going to see that she gets justice, for she is wearing me out with her constant coming!'"
>
> Then the Lord said, "If even an evil judge can be worn down like that, don't you think that God will surely give justice to his people who plead with him day and night? Yes! He will answer them quickly! But the question is: When I, the Messiah, return, how many will

I find who have faith and are praying?" (Luke 18:1–8, TLB)

How willing to hear and answer our earnest prayers is our just and loving God! There is more lack of faith on our side, unfounded as it is, than lack of desire to respond to us on our heavenly Father's side, just as Jesus taught:

> "Suppose you went to a friend's house at midnight, wanting to borrow three loaves of bread. You would shout up to him, 'A friend of mine has just arrived for a visit and I've nothing to give him to eat.' He would call down from his bedroom, 'Please don't ask me to get up. The door is locked for the night and we are all in bed. I just can't help you this time.'
> "But I'll tell you this—though he won't do it as a friend, if you keep knocking long enough, he will get up and give you everything you want—just because of your persistence. And so it is with prayer—keep on asking and you will keep on getting; keep on looking and you will keep on finding; knock and the door will be opened. Everyone who asks, receives; all who seek, find; and the door is opened to everyone who knocks. (Luke 11:5–10, TLB)

My parents and many extended family members started praying for my healing from MG when I was diagnosed at age fifteen. When I received my cancer diagnosis four decades later (four decades—count them), encouraged by my husband's prayers, we continued praying for my healing from MG as well as healing from cancer. Our prayers were not in conflict with seeking the will of God, for in all our prayers for healing we desired God's will first and foremost.

This is probably the most important aspect of prayer, something I cannot emphasize enough: I lay my life down at God's feet, bowing to his sovereignty, even while I ask my favor of him. I can truthfully say that several years before we began this renewed effort at prayer for healing, I had made the commitment to the Lord that if I could best live for and serve him in my state of physical weakness, then that was what I would choose. I still mean that today.

Nine months into cancer treatment, as I was going through the second round of chemotherapy, I realized that I didn't need to take one of my many pills for MG. I didn't need it because I was stronger. I have not taken that particular medication again since that day.

God can use whatever he wants to use, even cancer treatments, to accomplish his purposes, and he can work at his own pace to do it. God has graciously been answering prayers of forty-plus years for my healing from MG— in the midst of answering prayer for healing from cancer. Although I am not fully healed of MG, what God has done is a miracle nonetheless.

We must never give up on our problems or situations. We must keep surrendering ourselves to the Lord, seeking his kingdom and righteousness over our own will but remaining persistent in bringing our heartfelt needs to him. Unless he indicates that we should stop asking, as he did with the apostle Paul (2 Corinthians 12:7–9), we persist. That persistence in itself reveals our faith in God and honors him (Luke 18:6–8).

The point of prayer is not to get our own way but to move us into right relationship with God. God always hears and answers—according to what he knows is best—the prayers of those who fear and love the Lord. The key is to believe that our Father knows best.

I wrote this in my blog as I prepared to leave my sons, daughters-in-law, and grandchildren in California and go back home to West Virginia once all my cancer treatment was over:

> I pray I will not get overwhelmed with all that I need to do. My prayer times are often times of crying out to God, thanking him, praising him for his mercy and compassion, his goodness to me, for all the good things, and especially the people, in my life. Oh how God has poured out his grace and mercy on me! I just want my life to express his strength and joy . . . that is, that I would live my life as a song of praise to God, full of faith in him, bringing him joy, which in turn is my strength.

This does not mean we will get everything we ask of God. Not every sickness will be healed. Not every relationship will be restored. Not every reversal will be set right. At least, not in this life. And even if they are, it may not be done immediately. Yet, the choices we make as we suffer give us the opportunity to fight against this dark attack against God and bring glory to his name by praising him in the midst of our troubles.

"Therefore by Him let us continually offer the sacrifice of praise to God, that is, the fruit of our lips, giving thanks to His name" (Hebrews 13:15), "to the intent that now the manifold wisdom of God might be made known by the church to the principalities and powers in the heavenly places" (Ephesians 3:10).

We must stand fast, be strong in God's strength, and be persistent in prayer using the resurrection power he has given us to be successful in this fight against evil, however it comes, so that God's wisdom will be seen through us.

Part 4

Community

Chapter 17

A Community of Support

One of my best medicines is the family surrounding me . . . For them all I am truly thankful. We continue to realize that coming out here to live with our children and be with the grandchildren was the right decision. The little ones keep us smiling.

It was over a Christmas holiday with our sons, their wives, and our young grandchildren that Randy and I had to share the news of my cancer diagnosis. Stunned, our sons and daughters-in-law expressed their desire to be a part of the whole process of treatment; they wanted to help as much as possible. They asked us to keep this in mind as we made the decision of where I would receive treatment, because their personal involvement would be impossible if we were a continent away from one another. Our home was in West Virginia, in the eastern US, where we had lived for twelve years; our sons and their families lived in southern California.

In the final analysis, after much prayer, thought, and research, we decided that I would receive treatment at one of the premier cancer centers in the country, minutes away from the homes of both our sons. Instead of our children being a continent away from us, we ended up a continent away from our own home and work in West Virginia. But it was the right place for me to be for this long, difficult journey. I was surrounded by loving, caring family members in a place where I could receive the best in medical care as well.

A community of support is tremendously important to one in need, whatever that need might be. Mine was physical—with all the emotional and spiritual needs that attend such a trial. I required good medical care, but I also needed loving support during the long, difficult months of treatment. In addition to the love and support of family, I had many, many friends who supported me by prayer. Most of them lived far away, but they sent me cards, and gifts at times too, just to encourage and cheer me during those long months of not feeling well, living under the cloud of cancer treatment. During a difficult stretch I wrote in my blog:

> God has been good to me, to us. I have been bolstered by prayers and love from many people, and grace and peace from God. I admit I've had some emotional times the past few weeks, but nothing earth-shattering. I've

learned over the years to rest in the Lord a lot more than I used to!

It was a great comfort and strength to me to have my best friend and companion, my husband Randy, at my side, helping me make decisions yet not running ahead of me. Rather, he walked with me step by step. His love and support could not be measured. It was and is much more than I can ever put into figures or words. Really, that is what love is all about. My cup overflows with blessing because of him.

Another time I wrote:

There is one thing I will never get over all the days of my life . . . my great debt to love . . . all my life love has been poured out on me. I can only attribute it to the great mercy and grace of God. I view it as an expression of his love for me, that he has moved the hearts of others to love and care for me to this day. I certainly do not deserve it. But that is why it is the grace of God!

It is very humbling to know that not only family (both immediate and extended), but friends and even strangers (yet the family of God) care enough to pray for me and Randy. And some so earnestly and continually! It spurs me on to greater love toward others; to be more alert to the heart of God who loves so greatly that he gave that which was most precious to him, his only Son. This is a powerful ministry to me!

When we go through rough times, being surrounded by loving, understanding, and helpful people, whether family or friends, is tremendously important in making it through intact. We cannot do this alone. Nor were we meant to go it alone. God made us in his image. He is the Triune God—the Three in One—and he made us to be social, to need one another. We see this when God declared it wasn't good for Adam to be alone and so made Eve, Adam's soul mate and companion. Family, community, and church have all come into being by the orchestration of God, who made us to need and to love each other (Genesis 1:26–27, 2:18).

Philip Yancey, in his book *The Question That Never Goes Away*, recounted a story about a pastor who, when asked what the best thing a woman who was ill could have done, said she should have been a part of a thriving church for the past twenty years. The inference was that she would then have had a loving community of support to aid her in her time of need. Because she was not part of such a community, there was little she could do now but seek to gather that support. Of course, we cannot go back in time to build relationships within a church body, but the wise person will consider those words and start building relationships today.

The church was formed for our benefit. In its healthiest form, it functions as a family or a body, whose parts work in a coordinated manner. Care for one another should be a distinctive of the church. In fact, Jesus said the world would know we are his followers when we love one another (John 13:34–35). And love has many good expressions, one of which is coming alongside a suffering, needy member.

The church I am a member of has a "Prayer and Care" ministry. Men and women pray for needs of people in the congregation, some make meals and deliver them when a family is in crisis, and others visit shut-ins. There is even a woman who will joyfully do laundry for a family when needed! What great helps these are in stressful times. Many churches have similar ministries. It is important to let the church know when you, or someone you know, is in need, especially since we do not usually see each other every day to know how the other is faring. We need to inform others of needs that arise.

The church my parents attended would put on a luncheon following the funeral of a loved one of any member of the church. My mom was instrumental in organizing the women of the church to make this a solid ministry, taking it from a function of whoever happened to put forth the effort to an established ministry of the church to grieving families. As I recall, it even extended to community people who weren't members of the church.

I had the privilege of witnessing my mother serve a woman and her family of several children when she was ill and couldn't care for her home. Mom cleaned and cooked so her friend could rest and heal. This went on for several months, even when the husband became disgruntled with the church and ultimately decided he would take his family elsewhere. Mom continued to graciously serve that family. This was love in an apron.

Most of us can do that sort of ministry to one degree or another. We simply need to keep our eyes open for opportunities.

Community and support can come in many forms, sometimes from far away. Julia Francis called these distant supporters "our ravens":

> Despite my great lack of faith, the "ravens" sent of the Lord to provide for us began to fly towards us. Sometimes they came clothed as a postman, or sometimes as a fellow believer . . . I guess I was going to live Elijah's lifestyle after all. "And it shall be that thou shalt drink of the brook, and I have commanded the ravens to feed thee there." (1 Kings 17:4)[15]

Romania under Communism was not a friendly place for Christians in the 1950s and '60s. Julia's husband, Ferenc, a pastor, was arrested and convicted on trumped-up charges; he was sentenced to twenty-two years in prison. Julia couldn't believe what was happening. How would she live and care for her seven young children? She cried out to God, and time after time he brought Scripture to her mind and comfort to her heart. And he sent the ravens.

Then the unthinkable happened. Julia and her seven children were arrested and sent across the country to a ramshackle village of prisoners, dubbed

"Misery Village." They fended for themselves with few supplies and little more than the clothes on their backs. Cold in winter, heat in summer, and never-ending hunger were their constant companions. One of Julia's sons later wrote that they became quite familiar with grass, as their mother experimented with ways to feed them with it. But the ravens brought them packages, sent by people from all over the country, "with their love." These provisions kept them alive for the five years they were interned. Ferenc was miraculously released after seven years.

Those ravens, though miles away from Julia and her children, were "remembering the prisoners," and those being mistreated, as though they too were suffering with them (Hebrews 13:3). They were truly a community of support.[16]

When I was in California going through cancer treatment, my neighbor Louise, back in West Virginia, sent me cards regularly. She always wrote a note saying she was praying for me. She told me she did the same for other friends who had cancer or other illnesses. It was her ministry to us. Even though she and I were nearly three thousand miles apart, Louise's cards and notes encouraged me, reminding me that I was not forgotten back home. And of course, the value of her prayers for me cannot be measured.

During cancer treatment I went through many times of fear. When I was called upon to make decisions, I often did not know what to choose. That is when I sought wisdom from the Lord; the sound, objective advice of other people; and insight from

Randy. I depended on them all to help me make wise decisions.

Friends' and family's prayers buoyed me up. My children's care and concern surrounded me. Our grandchildren's vitality and unconditional love flooded me with renewed hope—and lots of hugs and smiles—daily.

This was the color and shape of my personal community of support. It was of inestimable value to me. However, it didn't spring into existence when I was diagnosed with cancer. Like the pastor's counsel to his parishioner, my community of support had been developed over many years of ordinary life. That is when relationships are built, in everyday life. Then when a crisis comes, those close to the one in need can surround him or her in an intentional way, holding them up in a multitude of ways.

Do you have a community of family and friends who are supportive of you, who care for you? Have you extended yourself to others in need? I've shared several examples of how people I know care for one another. What examples from your own experience can you look to for encouragement as you consider what it means to be a community of support? Community begins as we look outside of ourselves and deliberately reach out to others. It is never too late to begin.

Chapter 18

Finding Community

I realize that not everyone has a community of care and support such as I had. When people are suffering in some way, whether physically, emotionally, economically—whatever it may be—they need to build a supportive community around themselves if they do not have a readymade one. Family should be the first line of support. Barring or beyond that, the church, as the family of God, should extend helping hands first to their members and then to those outside their group, as opportunity and ability meet. It is worth it to let your church know about your needs.

In pursuit of a community of support, you as the person in need may have to go to a few trusted friends and share your need with them, asking these friends to walk with you on your journey and support you in various appropriate ways. You should especially seek the counsel of those who have been down the same path and come through intact, people who have a strong life with the Lord and can encourage and help you through the maze of suffering.

> Two are better than one because they have a good return for their labor. For if either of them falls, the one will lift up his companion. But woe to the one who falls when there is not another to lift him up. (Ecclesiastes 4:9–10)

Not only does the person in a crisis situation need to reach out to others, but those of us surrounding him or her need to be willing to lift up our companion. We know the verse that says, "Weep with those who weep" (Romans 12:15). Developing a mind-set and lifestyle of loving one another positions us to sympathize and empathize with those walking through a dark valley of struggle and suffering.

When we weep with the weeping ones, we enter into their suffering. That is a huge commitment. It is not for the short term but for the long haul. It will change your life to walk beside a suffering friend through "thick and thin," as the saying goes. It moves you from the state of onlooker to participant. It is risky, no doubt. But true community is all about our common need for one another, about love being lived out in everyday, nitty-gritty, practical ways. When we extend ourselves to others, though it may not always be easy, it will enrich our lives even in the midst of difficulties because God has designed us, in his image, to love one another.

Early in my cancer treatment I wrote in my blog:

> It has been three months since my diagnosis of breast cancer. My journey continues. It is not a path I would have chosen; I suddenly found myself here one day. Now I am surrounded by a great company of fellow travelers. Some have been here before themselves; others, though they are not compelled to walk with me, have chosen to do so, lending their support to me by prayer and encouragement.

People chose to pray for me, while others chose to get more involved, especially my family. But the one who is suffering must also choose to receive love and care. For some people this may be difficult; it is humbling. But receiving help from others is crucial for movement toward health and wholeness in the face of loss or suffering.

People who resist help from others do so to their detriment. They are the losers, and unfortunately, often their families are as well, because their love, offered in practical expressions, is refused. If we are tempted to refuse to receive love, we must remember that this love is God's love to us through other people. When we humble ourselves to receive from others, our lives are enriched, and those who give of themselves to help others are blessed.

I shared earlier how humbling it was to know people were praying for me as I struggled through cancer treatments. It convicted me that I needed to love others more. I could pray for other people and when able, do good to them, whoever the one in need might be. I would have missed those good lessons and life changes had I closed my heart to others who desired to do good for me when I was in need.

In the previous chapter I talked about being ministered to in my times of need and what I have witnessed of people reaching out to others in times of distress. This matter of community is a two-way street. When we are in need we humble ourselves to receive, and in the process we can learn to love others better. Being served can tune our hearts to be sensitive to others around us who in their turn may need our support one day.

We intrinsically know that those surrounded by a caring, loving, and supportive community have better outcomes physically and emotionally. I wrote on my blog:

> Cancer and MG are real entities which affect my life in some negative physical respects, but we are made by God to live, not just survive. In the most horrendous physical condition, one can be very much alive, that is, fully engaged in living life. You've seen it. I've seen it in others, and my usual inner response is amazement and deep respect for the one who shines so brightly in my vision. In my own experience with MG, I know this to be true. More depends on the state of our minds and hearts than on the state of our bodies. Anyone who has suffered anything in their body can nod in the affirmative to that!

How we respond to difficulties in life shapes us, either positively or negatively. It similarly affects the people closest to us. Much of life is what we make it. Without a doubt, though, it sure helps to be surrounded by people with whom we have loving and affirmative relationships. People are very important to the well-being of others. A humble heart that can receive and give back, along with good relationships with others, contributes very much to the positive attitudes needed to live happily even in the midst of suffering and trials.

Chapter 19

Support Groups

Extended family, church family, and friends are all potential sources of a caring community. So too are those support groups made up of people who, though usually strangers to one another initially, gather together regularly to encourage one another because they all deal with the same kind of problem.

In a support group, you will find people who are on a similar journey, many with wisdom and knowledge to share to help others along their way. They understand and can relate to each other's struggles. Sometimes just having someone who does understand your struggles and will listen sympathetically is all you need.

This was my experience. I still remember driving myself to the meeting place for the first time. Though it wasn't that far from my home, it was new territory, and I was a bit nervous. Besides that, I'd be meeting a group of people I'd never met before. That is always intimidating for a naturally shy person. To top it all, my muscle weakness made it difficult to smile and talk. But I was determined to go to this support group for individuals with myasthenia gravis, the closest one to my home. Maybe I could find encouragement among other people who had MG.

And find encouragement I did. I was amazed at the woman who spearheaded the meeting. She had MG? It was hard to believe; she seemed so "normal"! But in getting to know her a little better, I discovered she had her ups and downs and struggles too. Then there was the outgoing younger woman whom I thought was worse off than me in some ways, but whose spirit seemed indomitable. And the others were just nice people. Before I ever heard the guest speaker, who had new, helpful information for us, I was encouraged by simply being in the company of others who struggled with the same disease I had and were living life to the full.

From that time on, I have sought to be part of a local MG support group wherever I've lived. I have gained encouragement from other members and have been able in turn to encourage them. Through members of the group I was involved with in West Virginia, I was directed to a doctor knowledgeable about MG, with lifesaving results.

At the time, I had become so weak it was hard to speak, let alone be understood. I had great difficulty eating and swallowing and most nights had to sleep propped up in a sitting position to make it easier for me to breathe. We knew I was at the point where drastic medical steps were needed to improve my strength.

I was in desperate physical straits. I knew the slightest thing—choking on food, or maybe a virus—would send me into a life-threatening myasthenic crisis. I had to make a decision.

I contacted a friend from the MG support group and got the name and number of the neurologist at the university hospital some of them had spoken about so highly. More than one person in the support group had lauded this doctor's knowledge of our rare disease, MG, and the good results they had from her care and choice of treatment for them.

The university neurologist's office got me in right away, and Randy drove me to my appointment, a five-hour drive from my home. The doctor spoke with me and within minutes admitted me to the hospital for a week of specialized intravenous treatments. Finally, help was on the way.

Thankfully, I responded well to the treatments and within a week was able to resume a normal life again with greater strength than I'd had in months. Had it not been for my contacts in the MG support group, I would not have known about this knowledgeable doctor to reach out to and might not have had such a good outcome.

From personal experience, I can say support groups like this can be of great benefit.

Support groups can be found for almost every known life situation: cancer, other diseases, addictions, abuse, divorce, grief, and much more. Sometimes churches offer one or more such groups or give space for these groups to meet in their buildings. Finding a support group for your particular need could be as easy as calling some local churches or going online and looking up "support group for (name of condition/situation)." Your doctor's office may have brochures for medical-related support groups as well.

My experience of support groups is that they are led by people who, although they may not be trained in leadership, have a heart for and a vested interest in a common concern. A group of people with heart may trump one with slick organizational skills. Educating ourselves in our area of need is a necessary ingredient in successfully navigating times, or a lifetime, of trial. Finding others who can help and encourage you enriches the journey.

Chapter 20

The Gratitude Ingredient

Community is essential to one who is suffering. But as we have already discussed, there also comes a time when the sufferer must choose to give back to others who have poured themselves into her life. One should not remain a receiver only. She must become, in some way, a giver to others. Some people, unfortunately, live their entire lives taking but never giving back, but that is not the way of love or wholeness as a person. That speaks of ingratitude rather than gratitude

Gratitude is one of the most important ingredients for coming through suffering whole and healthy. Julia Francis practiced gratitude with her children in the privations of "Misery Village" in Romania. She wrote:

> With the ravens we received a task and job for us to do. We were compelled to thank God daily for his provision. We remembered daily

in God's presence those who had ministered to us, and in this wilderness lived closer to the saints of God in all the earth in unity than ever before.[17]

Caring for others will usually start with prayer, weeping "with those who weep" (Romans 12:15), and sometimes move to tangible help, depending on a number of factors. Even if you are still suffering yourself, love will always find a way of expressing itself, and in order to be a whole, healthy person, we need to love others.

I remember walking the halls of a large university hospital as a young person going to my medical checkups. I saw many other patients who were in what I considered much worse conditions than mine. I was able to walk, not bound to a bed or wheelchair. I was in my right mind. I struggled to do a lot of things because of my weakness, but I was functioning. I had loving parents and family members surrounding me. I felt that I had a lot to be thankful for. And I was right.

That perspective of gratefulness has stayed with me and colored my whole outlook on life. No matter how difficult my situation, there is always something to thank God for! This is more than optimism or positive thinking, which are centered in self. I'm talking about gratitude rooted in the knowledge and recognition of the goodness of God.

I previously shared that while in prayer during cancer treatment, I realized I needed to care more for others in the midst of my own cancer struggle. I could express my thankfulness to God and others for their care for me by praying for other people in need, even when I couldn't do much else for them. When I felt strong enough, I joined the prayer partner ministry at the church I attended while in treatment. I could certainly pray with empathy for many who were struggling.

Gratitude can and should take practical form. Writing a note of thanks to someone who has done something nice doesn't take too much effort, but it can be an encouragement to the one who extended herself for me. Giving back where possible is an important practice as well. Currently, though I am not a "food person" who enjoys cooking, I occasionally join other ladies in our church, dubbed "Angels in Aprons," who provide meals to families when they are going through a trial. Others served my family in the same way in the past. What a great ministry! Making a meal for someone else is one small way to give back for all the graces God has poured out on me.

We are all inundated with the graces of God, often expressed through other people. Sometimes we just need to lift our eyes, become aware of them, and respond in kind.

In all our need for love, care, and support from people during our times of crisis, we never want to forget to ask God to help us with wisdom, guidance, strength, and grace for all we encounter (Hebrews 4:16). He has promised to be with us. We can develop a keener sense of his presence in these most difficult times in our lives if we focus our attention on him, trusting that he and his Word are true. I have learned there is no other place or person to go to who can ultimately help me. Friends and family can encourage and give assistance in many ways, and I do not downplay the value and importance of the part they play in our welfare. But only God can give peace and grace to face whatever we need to face. Only he can do the impossible. He is the most important Person in our community of support.

Part 5

Purpose

Chapter 21

A Reason to Get Up in the Morning

I am convinced we humans are part of something much greater than ourselves; that we have significance simply because we exist, made in the image of God; that this life we live now is not the totality of life, rather, it is the prelude to never-ending life. I am convinced that this life is truly just the beginning, and the decisions we make and the way we live our lives now will determine where and how we will live our forever-lives. I have the certainty that we are here for a purpose—a purpose that is wrapped up with the greater purposes of God.

While going through cancer treatment I had times when I just didn't feel like getting out of bed in the morning, days I felt like everything was too hard and my life was useless. It wasn't just physical tiredness. I could stay in bed and rest and get over that. I'm talking about feelings of inner futility and inner weariness, feelings of "What's the point?" In those times, I had to go back to the roots of my life and remind myself of what was real, even when I didn't feel like it was real; I had to go back to the truths I knew, but which didn't seem true at the moment.

In one of my blog posts during those difficult days, I quoted from a little book by Malcolm Muggeridge, a British journalist and author. It was an address he gave as part of a lecture series at The University of Waterloo in Ontario, Canada. In it he talks about how in his old age, sometimes during sleep, he would experience being half in and half out of his body and have

> . . . the most extraordinary confidence, a sharpened awareness that this earth of ours with all its inadequacies is an extraordinarily beautiful place, that the experience of living in it is a wonderful, unique experience, that relations with other human beings, human love, human procreation, work, all these things are marvelous and wonderful despite all that can be said about the difficulty of our circumstances; and finally, a conviction passing all belief that as a minute particle of God's creation, you are a participant in his purposes for his creation and that those purposes are loving and not malign, are creative and not destructive, are universal and not particular. In that confidence is an incredible comfort and an incredible joy.[18]

My post continued:

> Yes! What more is to be said? I know this reality for myself. I have lived enough along the edges of life, being also the edges of death, to know in the deeps of my being the truth of both. We are but a breath. This makes every breath I breathe a gift, special, not to be taken lightly, not to be squandered. God has given me back my life so many times. To me, life and living mean loving God and trying—yes, trying, because I am still not very good at it—to love my fellow humans and give them the place in my life I reserve for myself. To love and serve the living God with all I am is all I want to do. To be "a participant in his purposes for his creation," knowing they are good, that these purposes are something much bigger than "me." This is worth living for. This makes me get up in the morning.

Even when I feel insignificant, or am tempted to feel that way, even when I feel powerless, I am comforted because I am part of something much greater than myself, as Muggeridge notes. I am part of God's purposes for his world. I can with confidence know there is meaning to my life, to my existence on this earth. From that flows joy. I am free to delight in God's good world, even when things are not altogether right in that world.

This confidence, this joy and comfort and meaning to life, does not originate with us but is a reality because of the Incarnation: God in the flesh, come in the person of his only begotten Son, Jesus Christ. When we embrace that reality, accept that truth, and receive Jesus Christ as Lord and Savior of our life, we can experience what Muggeridge spoke of.

The roots of my life, the foundations of my life, are set deeply in the Word of God and the God of the Word. Going back to my roots in God and his Word gives me perspective in the midst of pain and struggle and the fear of the unknown, for the unknown is only unknown to me, not to God. I can rest in his goodness even when I cannot see my way ahead. And I know, based on his eternal Word, that he is working everything together for my good and his glory (Romans 8:28). His purposes are being worked out through my life even in the midst of all this mess. I do not have to know how that can possibly be. I need only know it is so because of the character of God; he can be trusted. My faith is in him, not in my ability to have all the answers.

"His understanding is inscrutable."
Isaiah 40:28

Chapter 22

Choices

D r. Viktor Frankl, a Jewish psychiatrist who spent several years in Nazi concentration camps during World War II, wrote a book called *Man's Search for Meaning*.[19] In this book he shared his concentration camp experiences. It was there in the camps that he developed his "logotherapy" system of psychotherapy, which is considered a significant contribution to the field of psychological work.

In the process of explaining the psychological characteristics of the inmates in the context of the horrors that were everyday life in the concentration camps—hard reading about man's inhumanity to man—Frankl brings up the question of human liberty, the spiritual freedom of the individual in regard to his actions and reactions to his particular environment. Is man shaped solely by his environment, as some would have us believe? Or can a man rise above the influence of his surroundings?

Dr. Frankl saw firsthand that many men, even in the horrors and inhumane conditions of a concentration camp, could and did choose to retain their human dignity through the decisions they made. He therefore concluded that regardless of outward circumstances, every person retains mental and spiritual freedom of choice to become the person he or she chooses to be.

Alina saw this modeled by her parents and learned from them to choose what kind of person she would be in the midst of war and conflict. Her parents, Iraqi Christians, could not sit back and do nothing when their near neighbors, the Kurdish people, were hatefully mistreated by the government of Iraq. When they reached out to help those in need, their Iraqi neighbors turned against them in hatred and violence. Alina's family had to move away from their home for safety's sake. But they chose to continue doing what God put on their hearts, even though it put their own family in jeopardy: showing God's love to the Kurdish people. They decided to move with the Kurds as they fled from their homes.

"Each of us can take one small suitcase," her mother instructed.

Their friends thought they had lost their minds. Risk their lives to go to an undeveloped area of Iraq? Where electricity and water systems didn't function? And no decent schools existed for their children? How could they be so foolish?

Alina watched as her parents gladly went. "We felt that our whole family had an assignment and a purpose," she said.[20]

They had a purpose, a reason to leave the comfort of their home and all that was familiar. They did so in the face of fierce opposition, even violent opposition, from people who had been their neighbors and friends. They chose what kind of people they would be in the face of threats and fear.

My physical sufferings hardly compare with a concentration camp or persecution experience, but I know that what Dr. Frankl concluded, and Alina's family lived, is true. Most of us have seen it acted out on some level in others. We can choose to retain our dignity whatever indignities we suffer. In fact, our suffering can be the vehicle by which we rise to higher levels of moral attainment.

This is the experience of so many women I have talked with who have grown closer to God through their battles with cancer. It is fixing their eyes on God, the One who transcends all the smallness and pettiness and pain around them, which has given them what they need to persevere through the indignities and uncertainties of cancer. No one and no sickness can take that power of choice from them.

When we embrace God's point of view and his greater purposes, our souls are fueled to get up in the morning. God gives us the reason to live and not give up.

Chapter 23

Kingdom Big

"To live without hope is to cease to live."
Fyodor Dostoevsky

If the greater purposes of God in the world give us hope and a reason to live even in suffering, it's worth asking: just what are these greater purposes of God? Jesus spoke much about the kingdom of heaven and the kingdom of God (the terms are used interchangeably), in which God's reign is supreme, where his purposes will be finally fulfilled. These purposes are, as Mark Galli said, "nothing less than the salvation of humankind . . . in a rehabilitated earth."[21] All of human history is moving toward that great culmination. I contend it is worth the struggle to be a positive part of this great purpose!

A chain is only as strong as its weakest link. Our small home group, studying the book of Hebrews, came to chapter 11. In this "Hall of Faith," the lives of faithful followers of God who went before us are held up for us to emulate. I was impressed by the thought that each man in his generation passed down to the next generation the knowledge of God and faith in him. Like links in a chain, each man faithfully "held," even when desperate times came. Each link, each man and woman in their lifetime, was important in fulfilling God's purposes.

We are now among those links in the chain of faith. We have the opportunity and responsibility to pass on faithfully to the next generation the truth of God, with our words and by our lives. The generations coming after us are watching us. In fact, the whole universe is watching. Even if we feel we cannot offer anything to the success of God's purposes in the world, we can. By our choices and attitudes through our struggles every day, we can carry out God's purposes and bring glory to him while we are on display to the universe (Ephesians 3:10).

One man who did this without understanding what was transpiring was Job. Job was minding his own business, living his life, a godly man who sought to always do the right thing in the eyes of God. In fact, God himself declared that Job was a righteous man. Suddenly, Job's whole world was turned upside down and inside out. He hadn't a clue about what was going on in his struggle. But in Scripture, the veil is pulled aside so we can see the reality behind the suffering in his life, and to some extent in our own lives. What Job didn't know, but what we can learn from Scripture, is the tremendous battlefield we may become for the honor of God.

> One day as the angels came to present themselves before the Lord, Satan, the Accuser, came with them.
>
> "Where have you come from?" the Lord asked Satan.
>
> And Satan replied, "From earth, where I've been watching everything that's going on."
>
> Then the Lord asked Satan, "Have you noticed my servant Job? He is the finest man in all the earth—a good man who fears God and will have nothing to do with evil."
>
> "Why shouldn't he when you pay him so well?" Satan scoffed. "You have always protected him and his home and his property from all harm. You have prospered everything he does—look how rich he is! No wonder he 'worships' you! But just take away his wealth, and you'll see him curse you to your face!" (Job 1:6–11, TLB)

Satan figured Job would turn on God, blaming him and shaming him when all the "stuff" was taken away. God asserted that Job would remain faithful to him though everything he had was stripped away.

> And the Lord replied to Satan, "You may do anything you like with his wealth, but don't harm him physically."

So Satan went away; and sure enough, not long afterwards when Job's sons and daughters were dining at the oldest brother's house, tragedy struck. (Job 1:12–13, TLB)

Tragedy struck indeed. Everything Job had was wiped out: his livelihood, his fortune, even his seven sons and three daughters—it makes the mind reel. But God was right. Job remained faithful to him.

Then Job stood up and tore his robe in grief and fell down upon the ground before God. "I came naked from my mother's womb," he said, "and I shall have nothing when I die. The Lord gave me everything I had, and they were his to take away. Blessed be the name of the Lord." In all of this Job did not sin or revile God. (Job 1:20–22)

I can barely comprehend Job's loss and grief. Perhaps you can because of your own experience of loss. You know. Or you know someone who knows. The pain is deep and profound. The verse stating the fact of Job's grief is short, I think, because words cannot express such depths of anguish and pain.

But that wasn't the end of Job's suffering. Last of all he lost his health.

When Satan again came before God, he accused Job once more:

"Well, have you noticed my servant Job?" the Lord asked. "He is the finest man in all the earth—a good man who fears God and turns away from all evil. And he has kept his faith in me despite the fact that you persuaded me to let you harm him without any cause."

"Skin for skin," Satan replied. "A man will give anything to save his life. Touch his body with sickness, and he will curse you to your face!"

"Do with him as you please," the Lord replied; "only spare his life."

So Satan went out from the presence of the Lord and struck Job with a terrible case of boils from head to foot. Then Job took a broken piece of pottery to scrape himself and sat among the ashes. (Job 2:3–7, TLB)

When his wife encouraged him to curse God and commit suicide, Job's response in the midst of his agony was, "Shall we receive only pleasant things from the hand of God and never anything unpleasant?" (Job 2:10, TLB).

Good question, Job. Shall we take all the good from God's hand, usually taking those things for granted, and then rail against him when bad times come?

She was a young mother, lovingly caring for her infant son, her first child. They named him Robert, after his father, but called him Ricky. When he was only a few months old, his mother found him dead in his crib. He hadn't been sick; everyone was in shock. It was a terrible grief for the young parents. I heard the story when I was a young girl and was deeply impressed by what this grieving mother said about her baby's death: "The Lord gave and the Lord has taken away. Blessed be the name of the Lord."

A couple of years after Ricky's death, that young woman became my mother. I have never forgotten the power of her words or of her life.

It is tremendously important to grasp Job's, and my mother's, understanding of reality because this is the position we need to take as well. Job truly owned nothing, though he was the wealthiest man of his time. The blessings of God, by definition, are given as a favor, not an obligation, and in this world they are temporary. Job didn't deserve the good blessings of God, otherwise they would be called merit points for his good efforts—something he deserved or that God owed him.

God never owed Job anything.

God doesn't owe us anything either. Everything we have is from his gracious hand, undeserved by us. God has the right to give and to take away as he wills, and he is righteous in all he does and is worthy of praise.

But Job wanted to know why. Have you ever been there? I have.

Job thought he was righteous, living according to God's standards, and he was right. God said so (Job 1:8). Job thought that because he was living righteously, he had the right to question God, to call him to account when all these bad things happened to him. In fact, Job's worldview stated that if you do what is right, good happens; and if you do what is wrong, bad happens. His thinking was in step with that of his friends. Until, that is, he was himself struck down, and he knew he hadn't done wrong to deserve it. What was God doing?

Don't we usually feel the same way? Who is the first person many of us, whether followers of God or not, blame and hold responsible for the bad things that come into our lives? "God," we cry with Job, "why is this happening to me? Why are you doing this to me?"

> Then the LORD answered Job out of the whirlwind and said, "Who is this that darkens counsel by words without knowledge? Now gird up your loins like a man, and I will ask you, and you instruct Me!" (Job 38:1–3)

God went on to ask:

> Where were you when I laid the foundations of the earth? Tell Me, if you have understanding, who set its measurements? Since you know, or who stretched the line on it? On what were its bases sunk? Or who laid its cornerstone, when the morning stars sang together and all the sons of God shouted for joy? (Job 38:4–7)

God proceeded to compare his power with that of Job's, asking "Have you ever . . . ?" God had. Job had not.

God talked of the universe, stars, planets; the ocean depths and the gates of death; the rain and floods; the mystery of plant growth and the way of animal life on the earth. God is intimately acquainted with each facet of his creation because, well, he created it. He was there. He gave it his personal stamp of approval.

> Then the LORD said to Job, "Will the faultfinder contend with the Almighty? Let him who reproves God answer it." (Job 40:1–2)

There are some things we will never understand in this life because we are finite, the creation, and God is Infinite, the Creator. And God himself has told us, in his inscrutable wisdom, only what he deems necessary for us to know (Deuteronomy 29:29). I cannot speak to all the facets of suffering, only what I have learned over the years both through personal experience and from others who have written about suffering, especially in the Scriptures.

In the book of Job, God has given us a masterpiece of revelation into the mysteries of pain and suffering. God has also made clear to us who he is and who we are. We need to hunker down, with Job, deeper into these truths. Job learned the hard way, being brought up short and lectured by the Almighty God! But we can learn from Job's lesson, like the little brother watching from behind the curtain. In fact, I figure that is the whole point of the book of Job being written down: that we might learn and grow in our knowledge and understanding of God, ourselves, and suffering.

Then Job answered the Lord and said, "Behold, I am insignificant; what can I reply to You? I lay my hand on my mouth. Once I have spoken, and I will not answer; even twice, and I will add nothing more . . . I know that You can do all things, and that no purpose of Yours can be thwarted . . . Therefore I have declared that which I did not understand, things too wonderful for me, which I did not know . . . I have heard of You by the hearing of the ear; but now my eye sees You; therefore I retract, and I repent in dust and ashes. (Job 40:3–5; 42:2–6)

When we are confronted with the truth about God, as Job was, there is but one response: "I lay my hand on my mouth . . . I repent in dust and ashes." Though Job had some hard lessons to learn in his struggle to wrap his mind around all that was happening to him, in the end he proved that God was justified in his decision to test Job based on the truth of who God is. He didn't turn on God and blame him. He repented of the demands he had made of God and humbled himself before him, having gained a better understanding both of who God is and of who he was in relation to God. Job maintained that God was righteous in all he did, even if Job couldn't understand why all those horrible things had happened to him when he was trying to live in obedience to God.

The question remains for us: Will we learn from Job's lesson and our own trials? Will we let God be

God and be content to consider ourselves not God? Will we believe the whole record of God, that he, being all these transcendent things—all powerful, all knowing, everywhere at once, the Creator of all— is also the compassionate and gracious God, the God who is Love? Love personified in Jesus Christ, his Son. Love proved on the cross of Calvary. Will we embrace the reality that God's intentions for us are not evil but, to the contrary, good?

At the end of the book of Job, we witness the mercy and love of God toward his servant, for he restored Job's health and his fortunes:

> Then, when Job prayed for his friends, the Lord restored his wealth and happiness! In fact, the Lord gave him twice as much as before! (Job 42:10, TLB)

We too, like Job, are on display to the universe. We have the opportunity to prove that God was right in his wise decision to redeem mankind through Jesus Christ, as Paul said in Ephesians 3:10. Remaining faithful to God is paramount, therefore, regardless of our trial.

When the going gets rough, we sometimes glibly say to one another, "Hang in there." Yet that is exactly what we need to do! To hang in there is to persevere, to endure. That's what Job did. As James said, "Indeed we count them blessed who endure. You have heard of the perseverance of Job and seen the end intended by the Lord—that the Lord is very compassionate and merciful" (James 5:11, NKJV).

The outcome God desires for us is so much better than we can imagine. God's intent in allowing Satan to harm Job was not Job's misery and destruction. Rather, it was meant as a means of giving Job, God's follower, the opportunity to prove that Satan's accusations about him and about the character of God were wrong.

From the first lying insinuation against God in Eden, the fight between Satan and God has been waged on the turf of humanity. You and I are the battleground for God's honor. Knowing this should bolster our resolve and give us backbone to stand firm in the midst of struggles and suffering, not giving an inch of that turf to Satan.

Practically speaking, we have the opportunity to point to the goodness and kindness of God not only in the good days of God's blessing and protection in our lives, but also in the days of trial and suffering. Through Jesus Christ, we can offer to God the most precious of gifts: "the sacrifice of praise to God, that is, the fruit of lips that give thanks to his name" (Hebrews 13:15).

From Job's struggle we can learn much about maintaining our integrity and upholding the honor of God in the midst of our suffering. Like the men in the concentration camp and Alina's family, we have the capacity to choose to maintain our dignity in the face of indignities. Because in Job's story we have been given this view behind the scenes into the realm of spiritual warfare, we should remind ourselves that the things that happen in our lives are not just about us. They are much greater than that. We can gain perspective so as not to blame God for the bad things we suffer. We can remind ourselves that yes, there is a point to standing fast through it all—that we are upholding the honor of God and giving glory to the King who, as our Father God, loves and redeems us through Jesus Christ.

Though in this life we are the battleground, the war has ultimately been won. We must press on faithfully through the remaining skirmishes. Being part of this Something Bigger than ourselves should give us not only perspective and a new focus, but motivation to move ahead in confidence in the God who is the final Victor. I want to be on the winning side at the culmination of it all.

Getting up in the morning may not always be easy, but we have the God-given ability to choose to do it regardless of our situation because it's not just about us; it is about the glory of the King, our loving, gracious heavenly Father.

I am convinced that we are part of God's purposes for our world, and that those purposes are good and not evil. I take great comfort in knowing that when we entrust everything to God, though we suffer in this life, he will keep everything safe for that final day when we will stand before the Lord to give an account of our lives (2 Timothy 1:12).

I'm shooting for his "Well done," aren't you?

From the Author

It is my prayer and hope that this little book has been helpful to you in your own journey through trials.

Visit my blog, http://brokennesstobeauty.wordpress.com, and leave a comment to let me know how the book has helped you or someone you know.

Resources

General Christian Life and Growth

Hannah Whitall Smith, *The Christian's Secret of a Happy Life* (Uhrichsville, OH: Barbour Publishing, 2010)

Oswald Chambers, *My Utmost for His Highest* (Grand Rapids, MI: Discovery House Publishers, 1992)

Mark Galli, *A Great and Terrible Love* (Grand Rapids, MI: Baker Books, 2009)

Brother Lawrence, *Practicing the Presence of God*, retold by David Winter, *Christian Classics in Modern English* (Wheaton, IL: Harold Shaw Publishers, 1991)

Richard Foster and James Bryan Smith, eds., *Devotional Classics* (London: Hodder & Stoughton, 1993)

Richard J. Foster, *Streams of Living Water: Essential Practices from the Six Great Traditions of Christian Faith* (New York: HarperOne, 1998)

Amy Carmichael, *I Come Quietly to Meet You: An Intimate Journey in God's Presence*, arranged by David Hazard (Bloomington, MN: Bethany House Publishers, 2005)

Watchman Nee, *Sit, Walk, Stand: The Process of Christian Maturity* (Ft. Washington, PA: CLC Publications, 2009)

Living with Suffering

Kay Marshall Strom, *Your Life with Cancer* (Kansas City: Beacon Hill Press, 2012)

C.S. Lewis, *The Problem of Pain* (New York: Macmillan, 1962)

Joni Eakeckson Tada and Steve Estes, *When God Weeps: Why Our Sufferings Matter to the Almighty* (Grand Rapids, MI: Zondervan, 1997)

Philip Yancey, *Disappointment with God* (Grand Rapids, MI: Zondervan, 1997)

Philip Yancey, *Where Is God When It Hurts?* (Grand Rapids, MI: Zondervan, 1990)

Philip Yancey, *The Question That Never Goes Away* (Grand Rapids, MI: Zondervan, 2013)

Viktor Frankl, *Man's Search for Meaning: An Introduction to Logotherapy* (New York: Simon & Schuster, 1984)

Jerry Sittser, *A Grace Disguised: Expanded Edition* (Grand Rapids, MI: Zondervan, 2004)

Bill Crowder, *It's Not Fair: Trusting God When Life Doesn't Make Sense* (Grand Rapids, MI: RBC Ministries, 2014)

Julia Francis, *The Orphans and the Raven: You Answer the Orphans' Needs* (Bartlesville, OK: Living Sacrifice Books, 1989)

Ferenc Visky, *The Foolishness of God* (Cluj, Romania: Koinonia Publishing, 2010)

Nik Ripkin with Gregg Lewis, *The Insanity of God: A True Story of Faith Resurrected* (Nashville: B&H, 2013)

Samaa Habib and Bodie Thoene, *Face to Face with Jesus* (Minneapolis: Chosen, 2014)

Elisabeth Elliot, *A Path through Suffering: Discovering the Relationship between God's Mercy and Our Pain* (Grand Rapids: Revell, 2014)

Prayer

Richard J. Foster, *Prayer: Finding the Heart's True Home* (New York: HarperSanFrancisco, 1992)

Beth Moore, *Praying God's Word: Breaking Free from Spiritual Strongholds* (Nashville: B&H, 2009)

Philip Yancey, *Prayer: Does It Make Any Difference?* (Grand Rapids, MI: Zondervan, 2006)

E.M. Bounds, *The Complete Works of E.M. Bounds on Prayer: Experience the Wonders of God Through Prayer* (Grand Rapids, MI: Baker Books, 1990)

Madame Jeanne Guyon, *Experiencing God through Inner Prayer* and *The Way and Results of Union with God,* revised in Modern English by Harold J. Chadwick (Alachua, FL: Bridge-Logos, 2001)

Bible Study Helps

James Strong, *Strong's Exhaustive Concordance of the Bible* (Peabody, MA: Hendrickson Publishers, 2009)

William D. Mounce, *Interlinear for the Rest of Us: The Reverse Interlinear for New Testament Word Studies* (Grand Rapids, MI: Zondervan, 2006)

Oletta Wald, *The Joy of Discovery: In Bible Study In Bible Teaching* (Minneapolis: Bible Banner Press, 1956)

Online Resources

Bible Hub: http://biblehub.com. Search, read, study the Bible in many languages. This resource has concordances, commentaries, dictionaries, sermons and devotionals, and many versions/translations of the Bible.

BibleGateway: www.biblegateway.com. A searchable online Bible in over one hundred versions and fifty languages.

My original blog about my cancer journey can be found at http://jacquesjourney.blogspot.com.
My current blog is http://brokennesstobeauty.wordpress.com.

Endnotes

Chapter 1: Then to Now

[1]   Amy Carmichael, *Edges of His Ways: Daily Devotional Notes* (Fort Washington, PA: CLC Publications). © 1955 by The Dohnavur Fellowship. Used by permission of CLC Publications, Fort Washington, PA. May not be further reproduced. All rights reserved.

Chapter 2: Finding Hope

[2]   Oswald Chambers, *My Utmost for His Highest* (Grand Rapids: Discovery House Publishers, 1992), 137.

Chapter 9: Like a Child

[3]   Commentaries include *The Jamieson-Faussett-Brown Bible Commentary, Cambridge Bible for Schools and Colleges, Pulpit Commentary,* and others, found at http://biblehub.com/commentaries/genesis/3-8.htm.

[4]   Alfred, Lord Tennyson, "The Higher Pantheism" from *The Holy Grail and Other Poems.* Found at the Department of Rare Books and Special Collections, University of South Carolina. http://library.sc.edu/spcoll/britlit/tenn/highpan.html .

[5]   "Brother Lawrence of the Resurrection (c. 1614–12 February 1691) served as a lay brother in a Carmelite monastery in Paris. Christians commonly remember him for the intimacy he expressed concerning his relationship to God as recorded in a book compiled after his death, the

classic Christian text *The Practice of the Presence of God*."
From "Brother Lawrence," *Wikipedia*. http://en.wikipedia.
org/wiki/Brother_Lawrence.

[6]   Oswald Chambers, *My Utmost for His Highest*, 3.

Chapter 10: Types of Prayer

[7]   An excellent book on types of prayer is Richard J. Foster's
Prayer: Finding the Heart's True Home (San Francisco:
HarperSanFrancisco, 1992).

[8]   Amy Carmichael, ed. David Hazard, *I Come Quietly to Meet
You: An Intimate Journey in God's Presence,* (Minneapolis:
Bethany House, 2005), 63.

[9]   Attributed to John Flavel, a seventeenth-century English
clergyman.   http://www.brainyquote.com/quotes/
quotes/j/johnflavel399277.html

[10] Attributed to C.S. Lewis in *Shadowlands,* by William
Nicholson.   https://www.goodreads.com/work/
quotes/3154690-shadowlands

[11] Priscilla Shirer, *Jonah: Navigating a Life Interrupted*
(Nashville: Life Way Press, 2010), 75.

Chapter 11: Prayer: Just Do It . . . But How?

[12] The ACTS of Prayer are explained at http://prayercentral.
net/engage-me/ways-to-pray/pray-with-acts.

Chapter 12: Prayer as Relationship

[13] Oswald Chambers, *My Utmost for His Highest*, 90.

[14] Mark Galli, *A Great and Terrible Love: A Spiritual Journey
into the Attributes of God* (Grand Rapids: Baker Books,
2009), 26–27.

Chapter 17: A Community of Support

[15] Julia Francis, *The Orphans and the Raven: You Answer
the Orphans' Needs* (Bartlesville, OK: Living Sacrifice
Books, 1989), 47.

16 I first learned about the Visky family (Ferenc and Julia) through my friend George Deuel. He is involved with Christ Life Ministries, founded by our friends Joy and Graham Sumner. Their ministry raises funds for two orphanages in Romania, which my husband and I have supported for many years. These orphanages are run by the daughters of Julia and Ferenc Visky, and their husbands. On his numerous mission service trips to Romania, George learned more about the Visky family story. He shared this knowledge of them with me, and I knew I wanted to share it in this book. Through George I gained written permission from the daughters, Lidia Szabo and Maria Halmen, to tell a small part of their story. Julia's book may be purchased online. See the Resources page for information about Ferenc Visky's book.

Chapter 20: The Gratitude Ingredient

17 Julia Francis, *The Orphans and the Raven,* 48.

Chapter 21: A Reason to Get up in the Morning: Purpose in Life

18 Malcolm Muggeridge, *The End of Christendom* (Grand Rapids: Wm. B. Eerdmans, 1980).

Chapter 22: Choices

19 Victor E. Frankl, *Man's Search for Meaning: An Introduction to Logotherapy* (New York: Simon & Schuster, 1984), 74, 75.
20 Kay Marshall Strom and Michele Rickett, *Forgotten Girls: Stories of Hope and Courage,* Expanded Edition, (Downers Grove, IL: IVP Books, 2014), 131.

Chapter 23: Kingdom Big

21 Mark Galli, *A Great and Terrible Love,* 26.